MW00893833

Awkward.

WHAT TO DO
WHEN LIFE
MAKES YOU CRINGE

A SURVIVAL GUIDE BY

Sam Scholfield

ILLUSTRATED BY

Eliot Lucas

THE EXPERIMENT
NEW YORK

AWKWARD: *What to Do When Life Makes You Cringe—A Survival Guide*
Copyright © Samantha L. Scholfield, 2011
Illustrations copyright © Eliot Lucas, 2011

All rights reserved. Except for brief passages quoted in newspaper, magazine, radio, television, or online reviews, no portion of this book may be reproduced, distributed, or transmitted in any form or by any means, electronic or mechanical, including photocopying, recording, or information storage or retrieval system, without the prior written permission of the publisher.

The Experiment, LLC
260 Fifth Avenue
New York, NY 10001–6408
www.theexperimentpublishing.com

Many of the designations used by manufacturers and sellers to distinguish their products are claimed as trademarks. Where those designations appear in this book and The Experiment was aware of a trademark claim, the designations have been capitalized.

The Experiment's books are available at special discounts when purchased in bulk for premiums and sales promotions as well as for fundraising or educational use. For details, contact us at info@theexperimentpublishing.com.

Names, locations, and other identifying details have been changed to protect the identities of individuals. Because names and places mentioned are fictional to protect actual identities, any relation to real people or places with those names is entirely coincidental.

Library of Congress Cataloging-in-Publication Data:
Scholfield, Samantha.
Awkward : what to do when life makes you cringe : a survival guide / by Sam Scholfield; illustrated by Eliot Lucas.
p. cm.
Summary: "A humorous guide to dodging the social landmines that plague young adults at every turn: 24/7 social media, new work and living situations, tangled romances, big life decisions, and more"–Provided by publisher.
ISBN 978-1-61519-038-6
1. Young adults—Life skills guides. 2. Young adults—Conduct of life. 3. Young adults—Psychology. 4. Young adults—Social conditions. I. Title.
HQ799.5.S33 2011
155.6'59—dc23
2011019596

ISBN 978-1-61519-038-6
Ebook ISBN 978-1-61519-140-6

Cover illustrations by Eliot Lucas
Text design by Pauline Neuwirth, Neuwirth & Associates, Inc.

Manufactured in the United States of America
Distributed by Workman Publishing Company, Inc.
First published July 2011

10 9 8 7 6 5 4 3 2 1

Contents

GLASSBURAT
3226 WEST CARY STREET
RICHMOND, VA 23221

Merchant ID: 000000001584221
Term ID: 02372470
3762326595

Sale

VISA
XXXXXXXXXXXXX1174

Entry Method: Swiped

Apprvd: Online   Batch#: 001085
03/30/13   17:40:24

Inv #: 000012   Appr Code: 030815

Total: $ 13.60

Customer Copy

WTF is *Awkward* about, and why should I read it?

I am a master of stumbling into the awkward, embarrassing, nervous-sweat- inducing, stomach-cramping, stutter-causing hot messes of life. So, like peanut butter on the roof of a dog's mouth, I latched onto the idea of compiling the best advice I could come across to get us out of all the awkward situations we find ourselves in.

That's what this book is: a series of get-out-of-awkward-free cards, along with some agonizing OMFG-WTF-awkward anecdotes (most of them so cringeworthy, you'll be stoked they didn't happen to you). As much for me as for anyone else, this is a book to enjoy (in that schadenfreudish way), reference (when necessary), and above all use to avoid clusterfucks of drama whenever possible.

For example, how do you handle the super-awkward second, third, and fourth run-ins with an acquaintance at a bookstore, when you have nothing left to say? Or learning that your ex's new significant other is your boss? How do you backpedal out of saying "I don't have a cat" (in your get-kicked-out-for-having-a-pet building) when, as you speak the lie, it meows at deafening volume? And what's the best way to handle an extremely unfortunately timed fart, like when you're giving a presentation—or having sex?

Because—as my Mom used to tell me—we're all special, unique flowers, I offer multiple escape-the-awkward options for each situation. So, whether you're being shy, confident, or deliciously amoral (like escaping a lie with another lie), whether you're jonesing to embrace your inner douchebag or to be mature, when the Awkward Monster comes a-calling, you can choose an escape plan accordingly.

Much of the advice in here comes from my own experiences doing exactly the wrong thing, giving me excellent firsthand knowledge of what *not* to do. I also include the best advice I could find over the past several years through researching what the experts say, good old-fashioned trial and error (meaning that I've already made an ass of myself so you don't have to), and gathering "what would you have done?" answers from friends, acquaintances, and random talkative people in coffee shops, on airplanes, in line at the grocery store, and over drinks. The result is pretty solid advice on how to get through any awkward situation unscathed.

It's worth clarifying that while some things are horrifically *awkward*, there's a difference between that and *awful*. There are senseless, evil things in the world, and if you're talking about genocide, deadly natural disasters, or cancer, then stress over forgetting someone's name doesn't register in comparison. That said, although truly awful things put the little stuff in perspective, it's usually easy to see the stand-up thing to do when something awful comes up. The little things that sneak up on you (like when you ask someone when she's due—and she's not pregnant) can be challenging to handle on the fly, especially if you're trying to keep your dignity and everyone's feelings intact. This book deals with the little stuff.

So, enjoy. Hopefully by the end you'll be able to stab awkwardness in the face next time you get caught canoodling with your amour on your boss's desk. Happy potholed trails!

How this book works

I offer several different solutions for each situation—both because there may actually be several different paths you can take to get out of a particular awkward hell, and because everybody's confidence, moral compass, and tendency to rage (or run) varies quite substantially.

Through extensive research performed here at the Awkward Institute, we've identified the six most common options for responding to and escaping all types of Awkward Monsters. Here they are, laid out and explained.

(*Note:* Not all of these options appear in every situation's escape plan, so to make them more readily identifiable when they do pop up, I've included some fun icons that you'll see throughout the following pages.)

Embrace the Awkward. When you intentionally up the awkwardness quotient until it's funny instead of awkward, it shows a level of confidence that's quite impressive. Not only are you not freaking out or being weird, you're taking one for the team by giving everyone an out through chuckles instead of OMGs. "Embracing the awkward" can also refer to the "make lemonade" way out of a situation (i.e., it's happening, so just go with it).

Burn the Bridge. An option for those who don't care about the consequences and are potentially harboring sociopathic tendencies, this option is typically ill-advised, unless your aim is to abandon the relationship with your partner or partners in awkwardness. In that case, go big or go home, right?

Evade the Awkward. Lie. Lie some more. Be passive-aggressive. Run away. Hide. Basically, do everything but actually communicate in a mature manner.

Be Honestly Awkward. Sometimes the un-sugarcoated, unfiltered truth is the only way out. It's awkward, but it opens the lines of communication.

Be Cool. In other words, don't freak out. Letting your rising emotions get the better of you while in the midst of an awkward situation

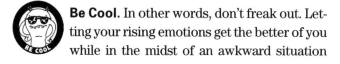

almost always equals "WTF was I thinking?" regret. For example, if you fart loudly during spin class, freaking out in embarrassment (whether that takes the form of intense blushing, anger, tears, or OMGing) isn't going to help. When someone freaks out during an awkward situation, it escalates the awkwardness exponentially and unnecessarily. In the interest of making an embarrassing or awkward situation as short-lived as possible, a good plan is to postpone your freak-out until later, when it can be fully enjoyed in the company of your loves-you-unconditionally-no-matter-what-you-did dog, behind your locked apartment door and away from public eyes.

Be Mature. Realize that it's not the end of the world if on laundry day, post-workout and sporting a huge zit, you run into your ex and their totally smokin' hot new significant other. Since you can't control anyone else's reaction to an awkward situation but yours, keep your reaction mature and rest easy knowing this is the option least likely to cause you regret.

Also, it's worth remembering that any sort of awkward confrontation resulting from a need to apologize (for a mistake made, for lying, or for something you did or didn't do) is unlikely to actually be as bad as you imagine it will be. By taking the mature route and sincerely apologizing (without groveling or unnecessarily apologizing multiple times), you'll get through the interaction quickly and everyone can move on. Even if it ends up being as bad as or worse than you thought, as uncomfortable as that will be, it will likely be over and done with quickly, and you can move forward without having the dread of the confrontation hanging over you. Yay.

You'll also see sidebars labeled **Dodge the Awkward Monster**, which provide helpful hints for not repeating the awkward scenario in the future (like banning cameras the next time you do something you shouldn't be doing so evidence doesn't end up on the interwebs).

I've also included a number of based-on-real-life stories throughout each chapter, both from my personal vault and that have happened to others. However, due to the fact that all are super humiliating and incredibly awkward, I had to change a number of details to protect the innocents involved (whom I'm sure would not want their hyper-embarrassing moments in a book). This is why I've called these stories **Something Awkward That (Might Have) Happened**.

★ Finally, this symbol indicates my favorite way out of each situation. It should be noted that my favorite way out is not always the mature way and that, with some situations, I have more than one favorite.

Awkward.

When your friends think it's funny to mislabel your boxes . . .

(page 54)

Necessary Uncomfortable Conversations (NUCs)

Sometimes awkwardness is the only option, despite our fervent pleas to be anywhere but in the moment requiring said awkwardness. Dumping someone, calling your exes to tell them you have an STD (because that's totally everyone's favorite conversation), or delicately letting your best friend know that their new lust object is a complete douche are all necessary, uncomfortable, and awkward conversations. And all require a certain level of savvy and poise to handle properly so that they don't turn into even bigger awkward messes than they already are.

Here are the very best ways to deal with the NUCs of life.

▶▶ You have a coworker or roommate who smells (bad).

Coexisting with someone who assails the senses every time you come within twenty feet of them can really put a damper on your daily happiness meter.

Sometimes there's a medical reason for the funk, sometimes it's cultural, and sometimes . . . ? Sometimes the person in question has an extremely loose relationship with the shower or a too-close relationship with their overpowering cologne or perfume. They may be blissfully unaware of the trail of noxious fumes they're leaving in their wake.

For all of these situations, if you plan on raising the topic because you just can't take it anymore, the potential for an extremely awkward conversation is very high. The problem lies in the fact that how someone smells is a personal and private choice (assuming the absence of medical problems), and when someone else says that they don't like it or it bothers them, a pretty common reaction is to get defensive. Another is to be embarrassed. Neither of these reactions breeds comfortable conversation.

To handle this, you could:

Be passive-aggressive. Put Vicks under your nose. Obviously cover your nose and mouthbreathe when the funk-embracer comes into the room. Mutter angry remarks under your breath, like "OMG, it reeks!" and "WTF is that smell?" Anonymously gift the smelly one with shampoo and body wash. Make a big show about your love of clean, unscented skin.

Generally, being passive-aggressive doesn't end well (because you're going to look like a jerk if you mutter and cough whenever their B.O. wafts over you), and it most likely won't work, since the person in question may not even realize that they're the problem.

Make someone else talk to them. In the larger, more corporate workplaces, you always have the option of lodging an anonymous complaint with HR or your immediate boss, and letting them handle the conversation. However, in smaller companies (or when you live with them and ask their friend to talk to them so you don't have to do it), it's highly likely the person in question will figure out who complained, and they may be pissed/angry/hurt that you didn't come to them directly. This could make things about fifty times worse, since presumably your goal was not to hurt their feelings but to find a solution to the problem.

Over-encourage on the good-smelling days. A favorite method of conflict-avoiders, fawning over how great the person smells on the days when they do shower, wear less perfume, or put on deodorant is a possible solution, although not a guaranteed effective one, since it's pretty likely the offender doesn't realize how much the other days are affecting you.

★ **Talk it out.** Although it's an uncomfortable conversation, it's far worse to let the situation fester (ha!) than to just have a conversation with the person about how their hygiene habits are ruining your life. This is also typically far more effective than hurling passive-aggressive hints at them. However, keep in mind that one of the reasons this is so awkward is that you're effectively asking them to change their habits for you.

So, once you're sure that whatever they're doing (or not doing) has become an obvious habit and wasn't just a one-off "oops, I ran out of time to shower this morning," pick a non-busy moment and ask to talk to them. This will set the mood for a more serious conversation and will hopefully indicate that they should pay more attention than usual.

3

Acknowledge that you realize this is a somewhat delicate and potentially awkward situation, but explain that you really feel the need to say something because it's affecting your daily life/work productivity/whatever. Then let them know specifically what bothers you—their body odor, their perfume, etc.—and ask if they might be willing to adjust their habits to address the issue. When you're working or living in close proximity to someone else, it's reasonable to expect the other person to compromise, just as you compromise your habits to live and/or work with them. For example, if they told you that your penchant for humming off-key show tunes really bothered them, presumably you'd try to stop in the name of keeping the peace. If their funk ends up being a medical or cultural thing, they'll explain at this point and, hopefully, understanding their situation will help decrease your angst.

In the case of someone who doesn't care they're affecting you, you'll have to suck it up and deal with it. This happened to a friend of mine his freshman year of college.

Something Awkward that (Might Have) Happened

>> DORM FUNK

My friend Tom's dorm roommate showered only once every couple months, resulting in a pretty intense funk in their room. Besides the body odor issue, the roommate's sheets would turn black with dirt and body oil. Tom tried gifting him shampoo and offering to wash his roommate's sheets for him (an offer than was refused with a "Thanks, but I'm good"). He tried air freshener, but the roommate complained about the scent. After a few months of avoiding confrontation (Tom didn't like confrontations), Tom finally asked his roommate why he didn't shower more often, and the guy told him he just didn't like showering.

Tom mentioned that the roommate's body odor bothered him, and the roommate shrugged and said sorry. Nothing changed. Not able to transfer rooms so late in the year, Tom invested in lots of (a different kind of) air freshener and left the windows open 24/7 until he moved out in June.

In cases like this, where the offender refuses to change, it's time to turn to the under-nose Vicks rub and hope that your time with them passes quickly. ■

Your roommate's/best friend's/sister's/brother's/mom's/dad's girl- or boyfriend just hit on you.

Sexual attention from someone who should be thinking of you as a Ken or Barbie doll (i.e., without genitalia)—like your brother's girlfriend—ranges from gross to flattering (depending on whose significant other they are and how attractive you find them—you're only human, after all), but is always, always awkward. Even if you find said inappropriate comments or gestures enticing and/or flattering, you can't, in good conscience, act on any invitations to canoodle. This person is with someone you care about. So, how do you handle it?

Tell on them. Telling on them is sure to cause some major drama and provide you with one hell of an awkward conversation to navigate through, especially if there are any underlying emotions (read: jealousy) between you and the person (e.g., your sibling, your best friend) whose significant other jumped over the do-not-cross line and toward you with a big smile and open arms. You don't really think your brother is over his junior prom date dumping him for you in high school, do you?

At best, you're confirming something they already know about their significant other, and at worst, you're starting some major inner-circle drama that can probably never be completely put back in the box (for example, if they stay together, your brother will forever forward know that his girlfriend had the hots for you back in Thanksgiving 2007). Then again, by saying something, you could be doing your brother a favor so he can bail. Where there's smoke, there's (typically) fire—i.e., if she's hitting on you, who else is she hitting on?

★ **Yell at them, but don't tell.** Your other option is to not rat them out but to make clear that their suggestion of a quickie in the bathroom at Thanksgiving dinner isn't going to happen . . . ever. You then have the choice of passive-aggressively insulting them whenever you see them in the future, ignoring them, acting like nothing happened, or ratting them out if it ever happens again. A potential con to not saying anything is that your brother may find out about the incident at some point in the future and be hurt/mad/betrayed that you didn't say anything to him about it then.

Go for it. All's fair in love and war, right? Just be prepared to cause some major emotional pain and to be disinherited, unfriended, hated, and/or kicked out. It's bros before hos, dumbass.

▶▶ Your boyfriend's uncle Ted or your girlfriend's auntie Kim just hit on you at a family wedding.

Ah, wedding impropriety. If moving their roving hands off your hot body or refusing to participate in any attempted flirtatious behavior isn't enough, your first job is to make the owner of the inappropriate hands or comments aware of how you feel. If they do anything overt enough to make this possible, say "Please stop" or "That makes me uncomfortable; stop it." If they deny doing anything or tell you you're being sensitive, you've got yourself a supremely awkward situation and several options for how to deal with it:

Make a scene. You could defend your virtue by making a scene the next time auntie Kim or uncle Ted tries something by declaring loudly enough to be heard by all, "No, I will not have sex with you." This will cause lots of family drama and is sure to make future family functions stress-free. Not.

Find a buffer. If they persist, simply find someone to hang out with at all times during family functions—your significant other, their cool cousin/sister/brother, etc. Chances are slim the offender will overtly hit on you in the presence of their family members.

★ **Tell on them.** Presumably your significant other has your back and will protect you from any and all discomfort at their family functions, up to and including telling the offending family member to back the fuck off. This is an excellent combination of evading (you don't have to confront the roving hands yourself) and dealing with the situation in a somewhat stand-up fashion (because you're letting your S.O., who presumably knows their family dynamics better than you do, handle the situation however it needs to be handled). If your significant other fails in handling things and/or protecting you, at least you'll be aware that it may be time to think about finding another significant other.

▶▶ Your friend is dating someone who sucks (but hasn't realized it yet).

There are several issues:

Do you say something when they start dating this person? What happens if you do say something and they end up getting married? What if you stay silent and your friend suffers a painful future breakup over their significant other's (S.O.'s) bad behavior (something you could have prevented by informing your friend of what their S.O. was up to)?

The problem with this situation is that your friend, who is heavily in lust with their new relationship, is not going to want to hear or believe it when you tell them that their newest bedpost notch is the devil.

When we've chosen someone to date, we rarely listen to outside opinions. How could the naysayer really know our new love like we do? How can they know how wonderful this new person is for us? We go by how we feel, not what we're told, and typically only consider that we should have listened once something bad happens and we're faced with the reality that our love is, in fact, evil.

So, do you say something or not? Turns out, there are pros and cons to both.

 ★ Say something

Pros: The most important thing is to have concrete evidence that the person in question is, in fact, the devil and to not base your opinions on rumors or vibes. After all (in theory), although the person may not do it for you, they could be great for your friend. So if you have no evidence, keep your opinions to yourself.

If you do have evidence (like the evil S.O. slept with their coworker last week, who also happens to be your other friend—I'll call that friend either Stacy or Ryan for ease of illustration), sit your friend down and say:

"This is really awkward, but if it was me, I'd want to know. Yesterday I talked to my friend Stacy/Ryan—you know, s/he works in [insert evil S.O.'s name here]'s office—and s/he told me that s/he slept with [insert evil S.O.'s name here] last week while they were working late. Stacy/Ryan was led to believe by [insert evil S.O.'s name here] that [the evil S.O.] was single, and Stacy/Ryan feels terrible about what happened. I'm really sorry."

Then it's up to your friend what they do with the information. Pressuring them to dump the evil S.O. will definitely get filed under "you don't support me," so stick with just passing along the facts and making it clear you support your friend's decision either way. Until your friend is done with the evil S.O., avoid offering your opinions or calling the evil S.O. any names—that way, your friendship can survive, even if the evil S.O. ends up being a major part of your friend's life.

For example, if your friend marries the evil S.O., as their friend, you need to be able to support them no matter what terrible decisions they make. When they commit to their S.O., it means that they'll forever be putting the evil S.O. first, and if your friend knows you're always waiting for the evil S.O. to screw up, it turns any small error on the evil S.O.'s part into an "I told you so" situation, which majorly sucks for your friend. Your friend won't be able to talk to you about the evil S.O. because they'll (correctly) assume you'll always have a biased view. After you've made your opinions clear, you can't take them back, so even if you tell your friend you support their decision to be legally attached to the evil S.O., your friend's awareness that you think their husband/wife is a total asshole will severely impact your friendship.

Cons: If you say something, you're a jerk for not supporting your friend and their decision to date the evil S.O. (i.e., you should support your friend and not undermine their decision by bad-mouthing their S.O., no matter what you "heard"). Worse, in the case of the evil S.O. lying and denying any wrongdoing (for example, the evil S.O. could insist that Stacy/Ryan is a slut who wants it and is mad because the evil S.O. rejected his/her advances—since the evil S.O. is true to your friend and your friend only), you'll get made out to be the jealous liar who makes stuff up to ruin your friend's life. Fail.

Don't say something

Pros: Since your friend is not going to want to listen to anything you say because they're in L-O-V-E with the evil S.O., you could just let your friend make their own mistakes and learn by experience that their S.O. sucks. Then once you're proven right, you can make sure to be there to pick up the pieces. This avoids all potential awkwardness with your friend . . . at least until your friend figures out (post–getting screwed—literally and figuratively) that you knew the douchebaggery their ex was up to and didn't tell, or finds out through the gossip mill how much you hated their S.O. and therefore were lying to them about how you felt the entire time they were with the evil S.O.

If you're not going to say something, it's probably best to play dumb and not talk about your dislike of the evil S.O. with anyone so the fact you knew about the evil S.O.'s douchebaggery (and kept quiet) doesn't come back and bite you in the ass later on. Basically, if you're not going to discuss the situation with the people involved, don't talk about it behind their backs.

Cons: You're a jerk for not having your friend's back and telling them what you knew.

When your friend gets totally peeved because they found out you knew and didn't talk? Be honest and tell your friend you didn't know what to do—you wanted to support them, and you knew that hearing one's newest love is a horrible person doesn't really sink in. It typically hurts the friendship far more than it affects the relationship with said horrible person. You're sorry, and in the future, you promise to report all rumors of douchebaggery.

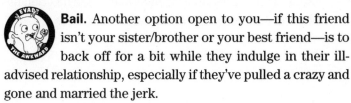**Bail.** Another option open to you—if this friend isn't your sister/brother or your best friend—is to back off for a bit while they indulge in their ill-advised relationship, especially if they've pulled a crazy and gone and married the jerk.

However, let's say the situation is more serious, and your sister/brother/roommate-of-four-years/best friend is in love with someone abusive or a drug dealer or something—in other words, someone that's not contributing in a positive manner to their life. If your friend (or sister/brother/roommate-of-four-years) isn't hearing any of your protests and is in a self-destructive spiral, you can back off, saying this as you do so: "I love you and I support you, but I can't be around you while you're in this self-destructive relationship. Give me a call when it's over, and I'll be here to help pick up the pieces and feed you gin and tonics."

How to dump someone you're dating.

Breaking something off, especially if the other person likes you more than you like them while you're just not that into them anymore (but you still like and respect them), can be complicated, guilt-ridden, sad, uncomfortable, and most definitely awkward, all depending on how you handle it and on their reaction. Here are several ways to do the deed, with varying levels of success in the non-awkward department.

11

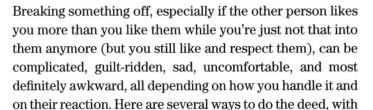**Fake your own death.** Perhaps it's easier to get over someone dying than getting dumped by them?

* **Upside:** You won't have to hurt them with your actions, just with the fact you "died."
* **Downside:** When they figure out you lied about dying to get out of a relationship with them, you'll at best have an extremely awkward, icy conversation to deal with, and at worst have a crazy ex hell-bent on making you honest.

 Lie and play the martyr card. Claim that you just found out you have a terribly virulent, as-yet-unheard-of, incurable STD and don't want to risk infecting them.

* **Upside:** They'll think you're super nice, albeit dramatic, for letting them loose because you wanted to protect them.
* **Downside:** Unfortunately, your martyrdom will probably make them like you more, and they won't allow you to break up with them because of it, especially if they're as into you as you think they are. Plus, even if you're successful in achieving single-dom, word will get around that you have some crazy new STD. This means that with any future partners who have heard the rumor, you'll have to explain that you made it all up so you could bail on a relationship (which will make you look like a crazy asshole and which will severely limit your chances of sealing the deal).

 Say you cheated and have met someone else (even if you haven't).

* **Upside:** This way they'll hate you so much, they'll forget about being sad.
* **Downside:** You're making them think they meant so

little to you that you betrayed them and their trust. This majorly sucks for them and leaves scars that can last for years. Plus, if you still like and respect them, why would you want to cause them unnecessary amounts of pain? Plus, expect your car to get keyed and/or all of their friends to treat you like the social leper you are.

 Pretend you've just realized that you're gay (or, if you're gay, that you've realized you're straight).

* **Upside:** They won't be as hurt as if you'd told them you met someone else—sexual orientation can be confusing.
* **Downside:** When they find out you lied about batting for the other team to get out of being with them, they're going to think you're a) bat-shit crazy and b) a total asshole.

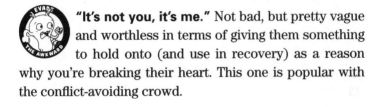 **"It's not you, it's me."** Not bad, but pretty vague and worthless in terms of giving them something to hold onto (and use in recovery) as a reason why you're breaking their heart. This one is popular with the conflict-avoiding crowd.

* **Upside:** You don't have to deliver the brutally honest "I don't like you anymore" line, and they don't have to hear it.
* **Downside:** There's not enough here to make them hate you, nor is there enough to make them satisfied that you're ending things for a good reason. Expect multiple reconciliation pleas, a lot of hurt (on their part), a lot of confusion as to what happened, and a longer-than-average recovery time. Ultimately, yes, they'll get over it, but if you don't give them a solid

explanation for why you bailed, you'll always be an unresolved situation in their head.

★ **Tell the truth: You're just not feeling the spark.** This is the hardest one to say (because it's the closest to home), and it's going to feel like you've kicked a puppy after your honesty-bomb has dropped. However, ultimately this is the best way to end something, especially if you care about the person, respect them, and want them to be happy again as soon as possible.

Delivering this news is a brutal undertaking, both for you (because you know you're going to hurt them) and for them (because it sucks to hear it), and there's no easy way to go about it. That said, there are steps you can take to make the dumping as smooth and respectful as possible:

1. **Set the scene.** Tell them you want to talk, and sound serious. This will help them realize that something's up, so they won't be blindsided when you deliver the news. Don't pick a public place— despite various opinions to the contrary, public shaming just makes it worse for them. Your goals are to make this as easy as possible (for them) and to show respect for the fact you have to do something shitty. Don't do it after you've been hanging out with them all day—instead, have the talk as soon as possible after meeting with them. Afternoons or early evenings are best: that way their friends can be there for a few hours afterward to offer support, and if it's a weekday, you aren't forcing them to sit through a full day of work after you emotionally destroy them. Doing it late at night isn't good either, since the chances that anyone will be around to be there for them go way down.

2. Think about phrasing. They're going to go over this conversation again and again, so it's key to make sure you get your reasoning across without saying anything that will make it worse. For example, some may take "I'm just not that into you anymore" and twist it into "I'd rather be with no one than be with you." This may technically be true, but presumably that's not the point you're trying to make. The point you're trying to get across is that you've realized you're not feeling a spark with them anymore, so instead of wasting their time and yours by trying to make something work that isn't going anywhere, it's better to end things so that they can find someone who appreciates their many positive attributes the way they should be appreciated. That way you can both find happiness.

Here are some examples of how to say this:

"I respect you immensely and want you to be happy, which is why I'm being honest here and ending things now before I waste any more of your time. You deserve an amazing relationship and someone who loves you."

"I've realized that I just don't feel what I should be feeling at this point in our relationship. The spark isn't really there for me, and you deserve someone for whom the spark *is* there. I like you and respect you, which is why I'm being honest here and not feeding you some bullshit line. Life's too short for things that don't move forward, and I don't see us moving forward. I'm sorry."

* **Upside:** You're giving them a tangible and honest answer to the question "Why did s/he end it?" when they ask themselves that for the hundredth time two weeks from now. This will lead to a speedy and healthy recovery. Plus, if you're going for the best likelihood of an amicable parting and potential friendship someday, this is the way to go.

* **Downside:** It's going to be hard. Really hard. Being honest is always really hard. Plus, you may be presented with some negotiation from them after you state your case: "What if I change this?" "Can we talk about figuring out if there's anything I can change that will help? I like you. I want to be with you." It's important to remain firm in your stance, however hard it may be. After all, you've presumably thought through your decision to end things, so in the interest of not dragging things out and making it worse for them, be firm, repeat what you've said, apologize, and then leave. When emotions are high, as they are when you're dumping someone, constructive, useful conversation is unlikely, so prolonging the conversation probably isn't going to help them, or you.

▶▶ How to "break up" with friends.

Ah, the friend breakup. Sometimes they're remnant people from a different chapter of your life (like college, when you were going through your punk-rock/drug-experimentation/slut phase), and you don't feel any kind of connection with them anymore. Or maybe they've changed (or you've changed), and you no longer have anything in common.

Often more complicated than hitting the brakes on a romance, dumping a friend has the potential to reach insane levels of awkwardness.

Dodge the Awkward Monster

Unless they've done something worthy of relationship implosion (like stealing from you or trying to seduce your significant other), don't be a jerk and end things with a text or email. After all, this person has been a part of your life long enough to have mattered and affected you. Over the phone is acceptable, but in person is best.

◄◄

Before deciding to cut things off with a friend, ask yourself the following questions:

Is the change in their behavior temporary? For example, are they acting out because they got laid off, their significant other dumped them for a coworker, and/or they're having a quarter-life crisis? And although they currently suck, if they clean up their act, are you down to hang out again? If so, talk to them. Express your frustration with their recent behavior. Ask if they're okay, because how they've been acting doesn't really seem like "them." Talking things through and calling them out on whatever they're doing that sucks is what friends are for.

If you've already talked things through and you have no patience left, let them know you need to take a break for a while because you just can't take it anymore. Losing a friend is a pretty big wake-up call for most of us, and it may help them shake whatever is going on and causing them to act the way they are.

Have they changed (or have you changed) so that the relationship no longer adds anything to either of your lives? For example, you've realized that their raging partying every weekend and the subsequent drama isn't isolated and is, in fact, a pattern—something that's been negatively affecting your life since you keep having to pick up the pieces the next day. Or perhaps they never actually seem to do anything but talk about themselves. Or perhaps you've come to realize that you're the one putting all the effort into the relationship—for example, you spent $5,000 and all your vacation time to go to their weeklong wedding in the middle of nowhere last year (forcing you to miss holiday celebrations with your family), but when you got married locally a few weeks ago, your friend was "busy" and couldn't be bothered to show up to your wedding . . . for which they RSVPed "yes." Friend fail.

 Let things fade. Have other plans when they invite you to things. Don't call them back. Fail to mention things you used to invite them to.

＊ **Upside:** If you don't care that much about their feelings, this is certainly easier than getting into how you really feel. They'll eventually get the message.
＊ **Downside:** If you see this person frequently, a confrontation about why you're avoiding them is bound to happen at some point. Since presumably you were trying to avoid a confrontation by avoiding them, being passive-aggressive will only make that discussion—when it does happen—even more awkward.

★ **Talk it out.** Although being honest and talking about your issues may result in more awkwardness (inviting conflict and/or being completely honest when someone may not want to hear what you have to say is never easy), holding up a mirror to their annoying behavior could be extremely helpful to them.

Sure, it's true that we're not going to like everyone and not everyone is going to like us, but when those friends that we used to see suddenly become too busy to see us anymore, it hurts. I know I'd much rather know what I did (or didn't do) to cause them to dislike me. Even if it's something I can't change (or wouldn't want to change), it's really helpful to know how people perceive me. How will I figure out something I'm doing is obnoxious if no one ever says anything? So, if someone gets to know me and wants to bail because they find my dirty sense of humor or the way I eat burritos off-putting, I want to know. Even if I end up feeling that, while they're entitled to their opinion, they're crazy and I'm not going to change, it's still helpful to have feedback.

That said, before you decide to air your issues, figure out exactly what it is that bugs you about the person and whether it's worth ending a friendship over. They're probably not going to react well to being told that their constant need to be the center of attention is extremely annoying, so be super sure you're saying something thought-out, real, and not based solely on your personal issues (like you're jealous of the fact they always get all the attention). If you figure out that your dislike *is* based on your personal issues, saying anything is pretty counterproductive, and it's probably better to just fade out of their life if you can't handle being around them anymore.

Delivering criticism, however well meant, can dive straight into awkward hell if care isn't taken to do it respectfully. First, mention to the person that you'd like to talk to them about something. Once you have their attention, preface the conversation with "Something has been bugging me for a while now, and although this is an awkward conversation, I'd want someone to be honest with me if I was in this position." Then be honest, with examples, so it doesn't sound like you're just being a bitch:

19

> "Although I've had a lot of fun partying with you, I've realized that I'm not that into it anymore. Watching you get blacked-out drunk every time we hang isn't

that fun for me. So, while I've had a good time with you in the past, I need to get out of that lifestyle."

"Although we've had some fun times in the past, I've realized recently that when you criticize what I eat when we go out together, it really puts me down. I don't need that, and I really just need to be around positive people right now, so I need to fade out of your life for a while."

"I've realized that you make a lot of racist jokes, and I'm really not okay with that. I've talked to you about how it bugs me in the past, but nothing has changed. It's gotten to the point where I can't handle it anymore, so I need to not spend time with you anymore."

Note that the last sentence in all of these is about what *you* need and what change *you're* going to make, not about asking *them* to make a change (e.g., you're not saying "I need you to fade out of my life"). It's much more powerful to let them know what you're going to do to change the situation than to ask them to do something for you.

Dodge the Awkward Monster

Communicating your issues is always far more effective when you do so in a calm, as-unemotional-as-possible manner, because this leaves little room for doubt about how you feel. If you lose your cool while letting someone know what's going on, they may think there's a possibility that you were just freaking out and will feel differently later (even if you were being entirely accurate about how you felt).

This conversation can also turn into the person outlining what they don't like about you, which is perhaps fair but equally awkward. Since you just dumped what's bothering you on them, take the high road and listen to what bothers them about you. Who knows? It may end up encouraging some very positive conversations and potentially continuing and deepening your relationship rather than ending it—honesty tends to do that. Of course, you could both end up hating each other instead. But you wanted to end it anyway, right?

If they freak out: Unless your friend is incredibly self-possessed, composed, and takes criticism well, it's on you to keep the conversation as unemotional and constructive as possible. If they totally freak out and you can't talk to them constructively, apologize for making them angry/hurting their feelings and bail until they're ready to talk.

Dodge the Awkward Monster

FOR THE EXTREMELY SHY:

For those of us who are very shy and view the world as one big festering pit of social anxiety, even the smallest confrontations can be terrifying. And when we're terrified, we're tempted to freak out—but freaking out escalates the situation into something far worse (and far more awkward) than it needs to be.

So, if you dread confrontation (and most other interpersonal interactions), the most important thing to remember is to calm down. Take a deep breath, stand up straight, and do your best to put all your anxiety, fear, embarrassment, and anger (and any other pesky emotions you may be feeling) in a box during your interaction. This emotional reining-in is something everyone can fall back on when trying to navigate the murky waters of awkwardness. It's a universally effective way to make sure things don't nose-dive when they don't need to.

21

Also, it's worth remembering that it takes practice to get the hang of handling awkward situations without freaking out. Expect to screw up. Embrace those screw-ups. You're human. Good for you! Plus, everyone loves hearing a truly, horrifically awkward story, so learn to love your mistakes and look forward to providing the entertainment at your next cocktail party. With enough practice (including practice at the little, everyday stuff that we all dread for personal reasons—and that might not even register on a more awkward-savvy person's radar), eventually even the most shy of us can build up our tolerance and bury our fear.

▶▶ Your significant other wants to move in together. You don't.

Cohabiting is a big deal, and although this is an awkward conversation to have, it's a necessary one. Just think how much worse the situation will be if, after saying okay to avoid the awkward conversation, you realize you can't handle living with them and break up when you're stuck in a lease together.

You have a few options for approaching this:

 Get them to rethink it. Do everything you can to make your S.O. not want to move in. Talk excessively about how you loathe washing dishes, doing laundry, vacuuming, and cleaning the toilet. Tell them gleefully how much pleasure it gives you to go number two and then not flush, pee on the toilet seat, or leave your fingernail clippings on the living room floor. Inform them of all your gross and/or annoying secret habits (picking your nose, farting, etc.), as well as your penchant for 24/7 video games or chick flick marathons or for harking back to the nineties and haunting online chat rooms—whatever will scare them the most.

Play the "I'm scared" card. Tell them that you've only lived with a significant other once before, and it turned out really badly when they had a nervous breakdown and murdered your gerbil. Therefore, you're scarred for life and aren't ever planning on cohabiting again, even after marriage.

Avoid the conversation. Suggest a vacation. Work a lot. Encourage them to work a lot. Go on a guys'/girls' weekend or encourage them to do so. If you're not around and/or they're distracted, maybe they'll forget about wanting to talk.

Get them to break up with you, so you don't have to a) break up with them or b) have the conversation about moving in. Don't return calls. Be unavailable. Tell them you don't feel like sex. Basically, be an asshole until they're so hurt and fed up they give up on you.

★ **Um, talk to them.** As potentially challenging as the conversation may be, if this person matters to you, I'm going to go ahead and guess that discussing what you're feeling could be a good thing and have a positive result. Yeah, it's possible that your significant other will have a "let's get on the path to wedding bells or end it" policy, in which case you just figured out that the relationship reached its expiration date. But if not? You've just successfully communicated, and hopefully the two of you will be closer because of it.

You just changed your Facebook relationship status and your new flame didn't, or vice versa.

Social networking has introduced a whole new bevy of awkward dating potholes to avoid, with relationship status updates being one of the worst.

Dodge the Awkward Monster

By far the easiest way to avoid any drama in this department is to simply make your relationship status invisible and not ever update it. By doing this, you can avoid the beginning-of-the-relationship awkwardness of deciding when to change it (and any "s/he did, I didn't" snafus), as well as the end-of-relationship "when do I do it?" debate about changing your status from "in a relationship" to "single," including that horrible broken heart symbol that pops up on everyone's feed, from your boss's to your great-aunt's to your ex's.

If, however, you didn't think of hiding your relationship status and now you're stuck in the middle of status indecision, here are your options:

 Hide your relationship status. Then claim that you recently started subscribing to the no-information-is-better theory and that you don't want to link profiles because you don't want your boss knowing about your dating life.

 Blame it on your roommate. They were using your computer and thought it would be funny to send your significant other an "I'm in a relationship with you" invite. Silly roommate.

★ Talk. Awkward, yeah, because you're either going to hear that your new love isn't ready to commit (at least not publicly on Facebook) or you're going to have to drop that bomb yourself. Consider this your first conflict together and treat it as a chance to grow as a couple. Or bail. Your choice.

You figure out that you and a friend (whom you like and want to keep hanging out with) have a crush on the same person.

Ranging from crazy to reasonable, you have many options:

Force your friend out. Seal the deal before your friend can, hopefully forcing them out of the picture. Then pretend you didn't realize they liked the person too.

Lie to the object of your shared affection. Tell your crush that your friend is really into someone else, thereby luring them toward you instead of your friend. Cross your fingers that your friend won't find out you're a backstabber.

Lie to your friend. Tell them that your mutual crush confessed their love for you last night. Then pretend not to see your friend's crestfallen face, you liar.

Make your crush choose. Talk to your friend and suggest that the best way to deal with this is to confront your mutual crush and make them decide on the spot whom they want to be with. (Warning: It may be neither of you. Also, this is super uncomfortable for the crush. . . .)

25

Decide who deserves your crush more: you or your friend. Talk to your friend and try to figure out which one of you likes the person more and/or who gets more play overall—the person who likes them more or who gets less should have a chance first.

 ★ Talk it out. Talk to your friend, acknowledging the awkwardness of the situation and the fact that you value their friendship. Then mutually decide that the best man/woman will win with no hard feelings after the fact.

Be a martyr. Back off and let your friend have a chance.

▶▶ The STD talk: "I have one" or "You gave me one."

A necessary awkwardness, this one.

>> "I HAVE ONE."*

If you're the carrier and need to relay this information before doing the deed, make sure you know the facts (and potential risks to your partner) before bringing it up. Many incurable STDs and STIs are manageable (herpes, for example) and are not the modern-day equivalent of leprosy that some seem to think they are. Not everyone realizes this, so there may be some (very) negative initial reactions.

Do your best to have the talk before the two of you are

* By the way, I am not a health care professional. Serious infections like HIV, syphilis, or hepatitis should be discussed with your highly educated and knowledgeable doctor so that you're extremely well versed in the steps you can take to avoid infecting anyone else.

naked and in bed together (that way, if they decide to bail, it's not nearly as awkward), and deliver the news calmly. Be patient and answer any questions they may have, and then let them know (assuming this is the case) that you're really into them and that, although you'd be very down with pursuing a relationship and seeing where it goes, you understand if the news makes them uncomfortable. Then let them know the ball is in their court.

Suggest they consult their doctor with any personal questions about your condition and the relative safety of pursuing a sexual relationship with you. Being mature, calm, and educated about your condition is the best way to alleviate awkwardness. Also, remember that while you may have come to terms with any potential changes to your daily life because of your condition, they are hearing this for the first time and it may take them awhile to process the news.

>> "OMG, I JUST FOUND OUT I HAVE ONE."

If you figure out that you've recently acquired an STD or STI but aren't positive when you contracted it, the onus is on you to contact all of your current and recent partners so that they can get themselves checked and, if possible, cured. Some infections take awhile to show up, so someone you slept with a while ago could also be at risk.

As far as awkward conversations go, this one is way up there.

The best way to handle it is to be straightforward, mature, and as unemotional as possible. Remember that the risk of contracting an infection is part of being sexually active and can happen to anyone, no matter how many partners they've had. Another potential stand-up move if you realize that you've infected someone is to offer to pay for their medical costs, especially if the STI is a minor one that's curable with a course of antibiotics. This is especially advised and decent if you had a "whoops, I cheated" incident and then gave your significant other something.

>> "OMG, YOU GAVE ME ONE."

If you figure out that a particular person gave you the infection, before freaking out on them, figure out whether they knew they had something before they gave it to you. It's very possible they had no idea they were carrying anything (yet another reason to get tested frequently if you're sleeping around). If they didn't know, take your antibiotics together and look at it as a bonding experience.

Dodge the Awkward Monster

Be sure you're accusing the right person of giving you an STD before you go ape-shit on them.

◄◄─────────────────────────────────────

▶▶ **You're at a party and just said something snarky to your bestie, Sarah, about Jane, your sometime-friend. Then you notice Jane is standing five feet away. You're not sure whether or not Jane overheard you, since she doesn't confront you about your snark. Do you say anything?**

Obviously the risk here is that if Jane didn't hear you and you say something, you'll be alerting her to the fact you were backstabbing her, and who wants to have that conversation?

But if she did hear you, why didn't she say anything? What's her angle? Does she not care (in which case you don't have to worry about it)? Or did she not say anything because she doesn't like you and/or thinks badly of you already, and overhearing you saying unpleasant things just solidified her opinion? If that's the case, do you care enough to repair the friendship?

Regardless of whether or not you like Jane, everyone knows that it sucks to overhear someone talk about you negatively behind your back. So unless you're really okay with being a jerk, chances are good you're going to feel remorse. If you feel bad, you're going to want to apologize, but that means you have to tell her what you're sorry for. Ack.

Here are the options:

★ **Don't say anything and don't worry.** Continue with life and make sure you're extra nice to Jane in the future. If she did hear you, your sudden turn from backstabber to best friend will potentially freak her out enough to make her say something to you about your snark, at which point you can apologize and clear the air.

Don't say anything, but freak out. Did she hear? Did she not hear? Is she acting strangely because she knows what you said? Let the neuroses and your assumptions build (i.e., wrongly assume that she's mad) until you can't stand feeling guilty anymore. Then call her at 2:00 AM on a Wednesday (or some other equally selfish and bad-for-her time, probably when you're drunk), be hysterical, and force her not only to hear about what you said but also to deal with calming you down.

Say something, but be obvious. Seek Jane out soon after the alleged overhearing and, without even trying to make things less awkward by starting out with "This is awkward, but . . . ," tell her what you said and apologize: "I just said to Sarah that I think you're a fugly beast. I'm not sure whether or not you heard me, so just in case you did, I wanted to apologize. It wasn't a nice thing to say." This is an effective, albeit super-awkward, way to clear the air, although she may question your brutal honesty as being in the TMI realm. Plus, if it turns out she didn't hear you, you just called her a fugly beast to her face. Fail.

Say something, but be normal. Wait for a good time to talk to Jane (like when she's not surrounded by fifteen other people) and set out to genuinely apologize for saying what you did. Communicate to her (with the intention of resolving the issue) whatever it was that caused you to backstab her to begin with (you're mad at her, you're jealous, she stole your boyfriend). Start off with something like "Hey—can I talk to you for a minute? This is awkward, but I want to apologize. I think you overheard me saying some not very nice things a few minutes ago, and I just wanted to say I'm really sorry for saying them and for the method by which you found out. It sucks, and I'm sorry." Then move into your constructive communication and resolve things.

From Jane's perspective, although it still bites to hear that you said something nasty about her, hearing you apologize is pretty nice and is a stand-up move on your part.

Dodge the Awkward Monster

Stop being a backstabbing bitch. ☺

You trash-talk a party (or wedding or some other event someone has taken much time to plan), and then find out that the host/hostess is standing right behind you. ◀◀

Hopefully you'll be able to tell from their facial expression how much of your dissing the host heard, and act accordingly.

If they're smiling: Smile back. Say hi. Express your thanks for their hosting. Don't apologize unless they let you know they heard you. If you apologize and they didn't hear you, you've just made awkward drama when there didn't need to be.

If their expression is unreadable: Smile. Say hi. Express your thanks for their throwing the party. Babble about something you genuinely like (and under no circumstances say you love something you were just talking about hating). If they heard you and want to make you uncomfortable by letting you know you've been caught, this is probably when it will happen. If, on the other hand, they want to torture you passive-aggressively for the rest of the party, you can either confess and apologize for being a jerk about all the hard work they've put in, or you can smile while you take the punishment you deserve.

If they're clearly pissed: Apologize immediately for your comments and for the fact they found out the way they did. Bonus points for saying something like "I've had a really bad week, and I just took it out on you—regardless of what I like or don't like, I'm an ass for not being appreciative of the hard work you've obviously put in, and I should have kept my opinions to myself. I'm very, very sorry. I hope you can forgive me." When apologies are sincere and demonstrate that you understand what the other person is upset about— namely, that you don't appreciate all the work they put into the party you're currently (not) enjoying—most people will accept your apology and move on, and the awkwardness will dissipate.

You overhear someone in your office gossiping about you, and they're not being very flattering.

★ **Break it up.** If you can, walk in on the conversation and join in with something like "It didn't really happen like that," and leave it at that. In one move, you've a) let them know you heard them talking shit and b) shut down the conversation—all without being bitchy back to them or allowing them to continue gossiping.

Be awkward. If you can't jump in with a well-placed conversational plug, you could also step in and stand next to them—as if you were going to join in the conversation—but stay silent. Again, it will be clear you heard them, but your silence will confuse the hell out of them and they won't know what to do. You'll have created an incredibly awkward situation that will hopefully scar them enough that they won't gossip about you again. Also, it will be fun to watch them squirm.

Talk to them. Finally, you could take the straightforward, communicative route: "Guys, I'd really appreciate it if, in the future, you could just bring any concerns or questions you have about me to me so that I can deal with them directly. Secondhand rumors are never totally accurate, and it sucks finding out people are thinking things that aren't true." Then just stare at them and wait for them to a) apologize and/or b) agree to not talk about you behind your back anymore and/or c) squirm as they lie and try to convince you that they weren't talking about you.

You're staying over at your girlfriend's parents' house for the holidays, and you hear her parents talking (negatively) about you through the wall. Do you say anything?

If what you heard indicates that they have some misconception about you—like they think you're a slacker because you wear flannel shirts and drive a VW bus—it's worth confronting them. If you like this girl, you're going to have to make peace with her parents at some point, so you may as well clear the air. It's far better to correct their misconceptions and make them like you *now* than to wait five years and have them try to dissuade her from marrying you.

If you say something: Be prepared to deal with some awkwardness upon confronting them. After all, they're going to be embarrassed. And since they thought you couldn't hear them, what you overheard them saying was probably pretty honest. Honesty is scary and takes a pretty high level of maturity to deal with, on both sides. However, if you keep your cool and approach the situation with a constructive, let's-fix-this attitude rather than with anger, it will be a lot easier.

> "This is awkward, but I accidentally overheard you talking about me last night. I'd like the chance to defend myself, if you're open to that."

The likely scenario is that they'll apologize about your overhearing that conversation, which will lead to a real conversation in which you can actually work through any issues they have.

However, if they're immature and aren't open to talking, you might be accused of eavesdropping while under their roof and told that their private conversation was for their ears only. This will make the rest of the weekend suck with insane levels of awkwardness.

33

If you don't say something: You can still take advantage of the information and try to correct their misconceptions through your conversation and actions over the course of the weekend. Hopefully by the time you leave, they'll think you're the bee's knees.

For example, if they said that they think their daughter could do better (or something equally as vague), you could bring up your plans for the future while everyone sits around talking after dinner: "I look at my current job as a stepping-stone for the future, and in ten years, if all goes as planned, I'll own my own company. I also want to compliment you on raising such a great girl—she's pretty amazing, and I couldn't be happier with her." Hopefully this will start a more in-depth conversation about what you want out of life and will give them a chance to get to know you better and to reverse their flash judgment about whether or not you're "good enough."

▶▶ **You're at your boyfriend's house, and his parents overhear you complaining about them. The next day, his mom confronts you.**

Apologize. Apologize again. Don't even bother denying it if you want things to ever get better with his family. When confronted, apologize, apologize, and apologize some more. Then blame your immature lashing-out on your fear that they—your boyfriend's parents—wouldn't like you. Emphasize that you love their son and you know how much he respects their opinion. Then tell his mom about yourself so she gets to know you better. Ultimately, she's concerned about her son, so if you can show Mom that you're a nice, respectable, stand-up girl, hopefully she'll forgive your rudeness.

Dodge the Awkward Monster

In the future, save your snarky comments about your boyfriend's mom's cooking or his dad's skeptical assessment of your career path for someplace where it's impossible for them to overhear you—as in *not* while you're sleeping over at their house. Duh.

◄◄

You just saw your best friend's girlfriend out with another guy, and they're clearly not just friends.

Getting in the middle of someone else's relationship can very quickly lead to a hot mess of awkward. But unfortunately, no matter how much you wish you could get out of the awkward position of knowing something that puts you deep into your buddy's drama by simply scrubbing your brain clean of the image, you can't. Here are the options for what to do:

Stay silent. Make sure the girlfriend sees you catching her with another guy, visibly shake your head in disappointment or shoot her a death glare (so that she knows you know she's up to no good), and then don't approach her. The aim here is to make her so nervous about whether you'll say anything to her boyfriend that she'll confess to him on her own.

Of course, unless your friend brings up the incident (or breaks up with her), you have no way of knowing whether she talked to him unless you ask. And asking lets him know you know something, which presumably you were trying to avoid by staying silent.

35

The unsaid threat. This is the same idea as staying silent but with some escalation. Once you see her, go and say hi and mention how you're going to see her *boyfriend* later that night (or the next day, or whatever). Then pause (for at least ten seconds—to make it both loaded and awkward) and stare at her and her date without smiling. Then walk away. The threat that you'll tell is clear, so hopefully she'll confess and/or stop what she's doing.

Unfortunately, once again, unless your friend mentions something, you have no way of knowing what happened.

★ **The ultimatum.** Say something like "I don't know what's going on here, but I'm guessing if [insert her boyfriend's name here] knew about it, he wouldn't be happy. I don't want to get in the middle of this, but I will if you don't tell him what's going on. I can't stand by and know my buddy is getting cheated on without saying something, so you have until Monday morning to tell him, or I will." If, by some miracle, there is a legit reason for her to be kissing and holding hands with the other guy (perhaps she's practicing a scene for a play?), she'll let you know. Follow through on Monday morning if your buddy hasn't indicated that anything has changed between him and his girlfriend. It will be tough, but wouldn't you want to know if you were the one getting two-timed? When you do talk to him, stick to just what you saw and refrain from any commentary or opinions, as these, however well meaning, don't help him figure out what is happening. Anything beyond "It didn't look good" is overkill.

Tell him. Don't worry about giving her a chance to explain anything, and just dive into their drama. Tell him what you saw that same night or the next day (couched either as "I saw Sara out tonight at Earl's . . ."

without any further details unless he asks, or as "I don't know what was going on, and maybe there's a legit reason, but I saw this," followed by the facts, minus embellishment or your opinions). Then let him decide what to do with the information. If you choose the former route, he'll ask her about it and they can work it out, and if you choose the latter, he'll have a bit more information. The former is a little less meddlesome and gives her the benefit of the doubt (however small that doubt may be).

Regardless of how awkward it is for you to bring it up, he's your friend, and therefore your loyalty is to him.

However, if she comes up with a believable excuse for what she was doing or accuses you of lying, your buddy is probably going to side with her. Unless she tells him the truth and confesses that, yes, she was cheating, you're the one who's going to look like the bad guy and the one whose relationship with your buddy is going to be damaged. If they break up at a later date, your relationship with him may return, but as long as they're together, you're going to be out.

You overhear a personal conversation (like when you hear the husband—of the hostess— talking to a woman who's not his wife about when to meet up later for a quickie). It's clear you overheard. Now they're staring at you.

◀◀

This is a nasty secret to get involved in, and ultimately, it's not any of your business. However, just by overhearing and seeing what happened, you're involved. Now you've got to make a choice about what you're going to do:

 ★ **Stay quiet and let them speak first.** If he offers some alternative explanation for what you heard ("We have an open marriage"), or merely hints at one ("This isn't what it looks like"), you're somewhat off the hook since you can go along with whatever they said and try to forget what you saw. Maybe it's the truth—maybe they do have an open marriage or some other arrangement. You can nod and tell them, "This isn't any of my business," and then walk away.

Judge them, but stay quiet. Stare at him and then walk away without saying anything. This is a somewhat implied threat that you *might* say something to his wife, which *could* cause the situation to fix itself without your direct involvement.

Make it clear you're not going to say anything. Before they start talking, jump in with "I didn't see anything," "Your secret is safe with me," or "This isn't my mess," and then walk away. Scrub your brain afterward and pretend nothing happened.

Get involved. Don't say anything to the husband but immediately tell the wife what you saw. You can't stand the fact that you know she's getting screwed and she (potentially) doesn't know it. Your rationale is that if there's an alternative explanation (like they have an open marriage), she'll laugh off what you saw, but if there's some funny business happening, it's better for her to know than not. By far the most inflammatory of the choices, this one is bound to place you right in the middle of Awkwardville, but in your eyes, it's the quickest way to "fix" the situation, if there's anything to fix.

Note: Getting involved should be reserved for people with whom you're pretty close, like your sibling or your best friend. However, if the married couple are friends of friends or once-a-year acquaintances, then it's really not your business, and you should probably just get very drunk and throw up on their lawn instead. Your incredibly strange behavior will be an indicator that something is very off in the world, causing them to question any lying they're doing to each other. The screwer will apologize, the screwee will forgive, and their marriage will be stronger for it—all because you barfed in their bushes. Win.

Communal fridge wars.

Whether it's space-hogging (does Sally in accounting really need fifteen yogurts?), food-kleptomaniacs (WTF happened to your leftover pizza?), or science-experimentation (is that leftover Thai takeout moving?), communal refrigerators are an incubator for awkward encounters. Sometimes the problems arise from your coworkers or roommates needing enlightenment about basic life skills (like how uncool it is to put the empty milk carton back in the fridge), and sometimes it's because they just suck (like when they put the empty milk carton back in the fridge as a vindictive "fuck you" or eat your pizza because it really doesn't occur to them that it belongs to someone else). Regardless, communal fridge wars—whether they stem from laziness, thoughtlessness, or assholeness—are extremely challenging.

At work, we deal with lying or lazy coworkers, crazy bosses, and slow computers. But nothing gets to us quite as much as someone not honoring the communal fridge code. Perhaps it's because eating represents our "me" time—which makes the refrigerator the closest thing to home at work—and to have that particular space violated feels pretty personal.

Roommates are even worse—there are fewer possible people to blame for fridge snafus, and when someone steals our leftover Chinese food after our long day in the office, it's very easy to become disproportionately angry. After all, we rein in our emotions and force ourselves to get along with our frenemies at work; at home, we expect to be able to relax and be ourselves. So, when that relaxation is interrupted by the blatant theft of a burrito we've been looking forward to eating all day long, all the pent-up rage we've been not directing at our douche of a coworker comes tumbling out at our unsuspecting burrito-stealing roommate at 7:00 PM.

Dodge the Awkward Monster

In the interest of creating communal fridge peace everywhere, here is a list of the rules we should all swear to follow and, if someone doesn't, ideas for how to *make* them follow (or guilt them into following), so that we may maintain peace in what should be a neutral territory:

RULE 1: Clean up after yourself. Contrary to what may or may not have happened while you were growing up, there is no refrigerator fairy who cleans out the sixty-day-old Thai takeout, the fermenting cucumbers, and that sticky puddle of . . . syrup? . . . that's occupied the back right corner of the middle shelf for the last two months. Unless you or your company pays someone to clean up after you, no one but you is going to do so. At work, this seems to be an especially problematic concept—everyone assumes that because it's not "their" fridge, "someone else" must be responsible for cleaning it.

RULE 2: Don't be a space hog. In a large refrigerator in a shared apartment, this usually isn't too much of an issue. Each person gets a shelf and a drawer, and you're done. In an office, however, where you may have fifteen people sharing a fridge, this becomes a nightmare. The easiest way to deal with this is to be as space-efficient as possible. Is it possible for Sally to double-stack her fifteen yogurts? Yes. Yes, it is. Now there's room for your burrito. Done and done.

RULE 3: Don't be a food klepto. This should be simple, but for many it seems to be quite challenging. For those who don't get it, here's how it breaks down: If it's not your food, don't eat it. If it has someone else's name on it, it's not yours—don't eat it. If you didn't bring it home from the restaurant last night, it's not yours—don't eat it. Also, regardless of how entertaining it may have been last night at 3:00 AM to take one bite of someone else's leftover pizza and then stick the piece back in the box, I think I stand for violated pizza owners everywhere when I say it's not, in fact, funny.

RULE 4: Don't be an empty-carton pusher. The easiest way to deal with this is to get one of those magnetized notepads with an attached pen so that when you drink the last of the milk (lips-on-spout-style) at 3:00 a.m, you can write "milk" on the pad. Although, yes, it will suck that you drank the last of the milk, it's not quite as frustrating and curse-word-inducing for everyone else as if you had left the empty carton in the fridge.

>> YOUR ROOMMATE(S)/COWORKER(S) ARE COMPLETELY IGNORANT OF THE COMMUNAL FRIDGE RULES. WHAT CAN YOU DO?

★ **Fight fire with fire.** If someone steals your burrito (on which you Sharpied "Susan's burrito—please do not eat"), put a foil-wrapped sock in the fridge the next day, with a Post-it that says "Ha!" or "Fuck you!" on the sock and under the foil. Or put a series of Polaroids on the refrigerator showing you and your coworkers spitting on a duplicate burrito and then rewrapping it. This probably won't change the food-stealer's habits, but it will be entertaining to watch them be disappointed their klepto habits have been discovered and/or try to figure out why anyone would wrap a sock in foil and stick it in the refrigerator.

Alternatively, you could just start stealing other people's food. If the klepto is going to disregard the rules, there's no reason you should make an effort to live by them. If you can't beat 'em, join 'em, right?

If it's a mess or science-experiment-with-old-Thai-takeout issue, simply remove the science experiment from the refrigerator and put it somewhere highly visible, like in the middle of the office kitchen table. Then wait for people to start freaking out about the smell. Tell anyone who complains that you didn't want to throw the experiment away for fear of upsetting whomever's it was. Hopefully this will embarrass them to the point where they'll fear the wrath of the collective office so much that they won't repeat their mistake.

 Get intense. Superglue a lockbox inside the fridge and put your food inside every day: peace of mind for you, scary-possessive vibes for everyone else.

You could also install a camera in the kitchen and waste a ton of time watching to see who the culprit is. Expensive, but at least you'll know who's doing the stealing, and you can find some other creative way to get back at them, like stealing all their pens or permanently lowering their desk chair.

If the problem is an empty-carton one, simply figure out who did it (easier with a roommate than at the office) and put the empty milk carton in their office or on their bed (if the culprit is a roommate). Bonus points for doing it on a hot day so the milk smell permeates everything they own. This is extremely passive-aggressive and will majorly piss them off, but it will also demonstrate nicely that bad things happen to those who leave empty cartons in the fridge.

Dissuade them with lies. Make an open announcement at the next staff meeting, or nonchalantly mention to your roommate and her boyfriend while you're all watching *Deadliest Catch*, that you're switching to a special diet of only stinky tofu, crickets, and raw okra. Then just foil-wrap everything you buy and write your name on it, along with a list of made-up, the-more-revolting-the-better ingredients.

Freak out. Communicate your frustration to as many people as possible, as often as possible. Unfortunate as it is true, unless you make a big deal about your frustrations and point out specific grievances, things may not change. Refrigerators seem to be places where we all assume that we're not doing anything wrong and that any grievances filed aren't our fault: i.e., we totally didn't see the writing on Susan's burrito—we thought it was left over from the company lunch yesterday. And the milk? There was *totally* some left when we put it back.

★ **Nicely ask the perpetrator to stop.** Although this requires actual confrontation and is therefore potentially more awkward than taking the passive-aggressive route, it may be the only way to see a change. Sometimes people are just thoughtless and don't realize they're offending you, and sometimes they just suck. Either way, in order to make anything happen, you need to point out exactly what bothered you (the thing growing in your roommate's takeout ate your baby carrots) and ask for a specific change in behavior in the future (could your roommate please discard their takeout when it's clearly harboring several billion colonies of bacteria?)

In other words, before going aggro about your missing pizza, have a polite conversation and ask the perp to stop. For example:

"So, I noticed that my leftover pizza isn't in the fridge anymore. In the future, could you please ask me before eating my leftovers? I was saving that for dinner tonight."

"So, I noticed that the OJ carton was empty when I pulled it out this morning. It was full when I had some yesterday. I'd really appreciate it if the next time you finish something you could write down that we need more and recycle the carton."

Most unintentional perps will offer to buy you dinner to make up for it (or at least sincerely apologize and not repeat their mistake). Problem solved.

▶▶ How do you say no when you throw a party with a limited guest list and your coworker finds out and asks to be invited?

★ **Suck it up and compromise.** Since telling the person you work with every day that they don't make your "friend" cut is out of the question, a little compromise is in order. Explain that the guest list is set for this one because of your limited space, but you'll definitely put them on the list for the next one. Of course, you'll need to make good on this offer if you don't want to have to be super careful about talking about your social life at work (and who wants that?).

Although it's totally awkward that this person basically invited themselves to your party, because of your proximity to them, the potential for daily work awkwardness far outweighs the potential awkwardness of just inviting them to your next party to get them off your back. And really, is it that big of a deal? They're one person. And they might even bring beer.

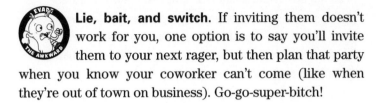 **Lie, bait, and switch.** If inviting them doesn't work for you, one option is to say you'll invite them to your next rager, but then plan that party when you know your coworker can't come (like when they're out of town on business). Go-go-super-bitch!

You're getting married and had to severely slash the guest list because, as it turns out, weddings are crazy expensive. You're out with a group of friends, two of whom are invited, the rest of whom aren't. One of the invited starts gushing about how much she liked your invitations, and the uninvited are now giving you WTF looks.

Since the cat just tumbled, meowing and hissing, out of the proverbial bag, you need to deal with the aftermath as graciously as possible. It's unlikely that your uninvited friends wouldn't have eventually found out about the wedding (and the fact they aren't invited), so now's your chance to jump in and soothe any hurt feelings—in person and early on.

Start by apologizing to the uninviteds for their finding out like this. Let them know that you've been agonizing over your guest list since the engagement and that, once you figured out your budget, you had to cut your list from three hundred to fifty. As a result, many, many people that you would have loved to be there can't be because you can't afford it. Look super bummed.

If you get attitude, stand your ground. Although it's tough, unless you're rolling in Benjamins or are on one of those reality shows where they pay for your wedding, guest list cuts are a necessary reality.

Dodge the Awkward Monster

If you're bummed about your guest list slashing and can tell others are upset that they can't come, consider having a pre- or post-wedding night out (where everyone buys their own drinks) and inviting everyone you want. This lets you celebrate with everyone without having to worry about going $100K in debt.

In the future, if you know that you're going to be mixing inviteds and uninviteds while out, call them all ahead of time to caution the inviteds against talking about the wedding and to tell the uninviteds about your guest list situation so they know you didn't forget about them—this will go a long way toward smoothing over hurt feelings.

 You're out with a group of friends who all make more money than you, and you deliberately order the cheapest thing on the menu because you're broke. When the bill comes, they want to split it evenly.

 Agree but be bitter. Agree to split the bill but silently resent them for not being more sympathetic to your financial plight. Then pull a passive-aggressive-loser move and make them feel bad the next time by only ordering water and saying that you spent your monthly allowance on the last bill you all split, so you're going hungry tonight instead of eating.

 Walk out on the bill. You'll lose them as friends, but at least you'll be a few dollars less poor.

Make a big deal out of it. Immediately follow your order of salad and water with an announcement to the group that you're broke and that's why you're ordering rabbit food for dinner. Then to erase the "I feel sorry for you" looks on everyone's faces (including the waitress's), make a joke about how you're happy everyone else is drinking to celebrate your pity party, and if anyone wants to share you'll gladly accept handouts. Note that if you pull this stunt on a frequent basis, your asking for handouts will get old.

★ **Come clean.** When the bill comes and the suggestion is put forward to split the bill evenly, apologetically explain that you just can't afford to do that (hence the rabbit food order). If pushed, stand your ground. As long as you didn't drink the shared table wine or eat more than a bite of the shared appetizers, it's unlikely anyone will have an issue.

Professionally awkward: How do you handle those (really awkward) "networking" events your school sets up, where you're not supposed to fish for a job but that's the whole reason for going?

When you're supposed to network without networking, it definitely creates an awkward environment. You know you're there for a job and they know you're there for a job, but everyone's supposed to operate as if they're not fully aware of the actual intent of the open bar/Hello-my-name-is event.

Here are some ideas:

Do your homework. Read up on five or ten people who will be there and what their companies do. Create a list of interesting, somewhat thought-provoking, non-generic (so you'll be remembered) questions about them individually. For example:

"What was it like to travel in Papua New Guinea for that project last year?"

"I'll admit I did a little Google stalking before I came here, and am very curious how you went from an undergrad degree in art to holding what I think must be one of the greatest jobs in the world—being [insert job title] for [insert their company]."

Focus on being flattering, admitting any awkward facts (like the fact that you cyber-stalked them), and getting to know them beyond just the standard, boring questions of "What's your job like?" and "How many years have you worked for [insert company name]?" Your exuberance and excitement for them and their company will be clearly evident (by your research in preparation for meeting them), and your interesting questions will make you stand out from the crowd.

As a bonus, interesting questions will not only be a breath of fresh air and fun for them to answer, but will also often lead to entertaining, memorable conversations in which they'll get to know you, too. After that, exchanging contact information at the end of the ten-minute bonding session will be a very natural progression of the conversation. Then you can initiate the standard follow-up exchange with a thank-you, a mention of what they mentioned (your coming in to meet their head of HR), and a genuine statement of how much you enjoyed meeting them.

48 **Find something to talk about that's not "I need a job" focused.** Demonstrating confidence by easily starting a conversation and keeping it going is a huge plus, and will serve you well for almost any job that requires interaction with anyone else. The person who has the social skills to be comfortable in an uncomfortable situation (like forced networking) is going to rate very highly in recruiters' estimations. So, how do you do this?

At a networking event like the ones colleges set up, one of the best ways to start a conversation (if you haven't done your homework and have questions prepared) is to make a wry observation about the awkwardness of said event and make your targeted contact laugh. Find your target at the bar or at the snack table and hang out for a minute, doing something else so they don't think you're there to talk to them (watch the room, grab some M&M's or a drink, etc.). Position your body sideways so you're standing next to them and not facing them (this is way more casual, easygoing, and natural if you're going to "fall into conversation") and say: "So . . . are all these events this awkward?"

They'll laugh and turn to face you, at which point you can talk about the awkwardness: "I was instructed upon arriving that I shouldn't fish for a job or hand out my résumé but that the whole point of coming here was to hand out my résumé and fish for a job. Everyone knows I'm here for a job, and I know you're all here to potentially find an addition to your company. How is anyone supposed to talk when there's a giant elephant in the room? It's so awkward!"

Then ask for advice on how to handle the awkwardness. Ask what the best conversation they've had at a networking event was. Hopefully the subject of that conversation will be something interesting you can ask questions about. Tell a funny story about how you can handle other awkward situations (like how your roommate is a nudist and walked in on your study group in the living room the other day), but the right approach to this event eludes you. As the conversation naturally progresses, you can start asking more personal questions: What company do they represent? What do they do? Which college have they liked the best so far?

Focus on them and their interests. Eventually, once you've won them over, they'll ask about you. If you keep up your confidence and make them laugh, you'll end up with a business card at the end of the conversation, and potentially a job offer.

 Your roommate's friend has been crashing on the living room couch for the last two months, and you're over not having a place to watch TV at night.

This is a slightly less awkward situation than if it was *your* friend crashing—after all, your roommate will have to be the one to kick their friend off the couch, not you. However, if your roommate isn't annoyed yet and sees no problem with their friend continuing to occupy your favorite after-work spot in front of the TV, awkwardness ensues.

If a simple "Hey dude—WTF is up with your friend? He's been here for, like, two months. Please make my day and tell me he's getting his own place soon" doesn't spur your roommate into kicking the freeloader to the curb and onto another couch somewhere else, it's time to identify what exactly is itching your "this bugs the shit out of me" bone. To help you compose a laundry list of items to complain about to your roommate, here are some questions to consider:

* Is the freeloader eating your food?
* Is the freeloader hogging the shower (if you all share a bathroom)?
* Does the freeloader make a mess and then not clean up?
* Is the freeloader's stuff everywhere, so you keep tripping over it?
* Does the freeloader share the couch when they're not sleeping on it? As in, is anyone else able to

enjoy the couch during the day, or is it constantly covered with their stuff?

Figuring out exactly what about the freeloader is pissing you off can do wonders for getting your roommate to see the light and do something about the situation, especially if your incessant nagging is even more annoying than their couch-surfing friend.

If the freeloader has nowhere else to go and you don't want to be the one who makes them homeless, laying down some ground rules and asking the freeloader to pitch in for their share of rent, bills, and food may assuage some of your angst. After all, you're paying rent and didn't sign up for this.

Your friend, who just moved and is "feeling out the city" on your couch, has been doing so for three months—when it was only supposed to be for a week.

Dodge the Awkward Monster

To prevent this situation in the future, before the friend arrives, decide upon an expiration date for their couch occupation. This way, you'll have some ground to stand on if they overstay their welcome.

Here are some options for dealing with your couch hogger:

You're done. If you're just over them and don't care if you ever see their freeloading face again— after all, who extends a week into three months?— you could burn the bridge with a flamethrower by announcing, out of the blue (and with no previous complaints about their behavior), that they have an hour to get out or you're going to call the cops and report them as a trespasser. You get bonus points for being melodramatic and alerting them to your change of heart by pulling the pillows out from underneath them while they're taking their afternoon nap.

Be passive-aggressive. If you're feeling a bit less like a giant jerk but don't want to deal with the confrontation, you could take the passive-aggressive route and loudly sigh whenever you "accidentally" trip over something of theirs in the living room, ignore them when you're in the same room, change the channel to whatever you want to watch while they're watching TV, and/or pretend to be confused by where all the leftovers went.

Be an under-the-radar douche. Straddle the fence of communication and passive-aggressiveness by letting them know everything they're doing that bugs you, but without actually offering any sort of solution or asking them to leave. This will make them feel really bad for putting you out, and awkward because you're being "nice" by letting them stay even though they're obviously pissing you off.

For example:

"God! I hate it when the dishes sit in the sink for two days—do you know who did this?" (when you're very aware it was them that did it, and they're very aware that you're aware)

"Oh, don't worry about cleaning your stuff off the couch. I'll do it."

Expect lots of favors if they stay, like coming home to find the bathroom scrubbed top to bottom or your refrigerator cleaned and organized.

★ **Talk about it.** If you're feeling mature, you could sit the person down and let them know that although you've enjoyed having them around, if they need more time to find a place of their own, they're going to need to start pitching in for rent, bills, food, cleaning, etc. You just can't afford to keep floating them.

Pick a time when neither of you is in the middle of something else, like when they're reading a book on the couch and you just got home from work. Bring it up by saying something like this: "So, I love having you here, but I realized that my grocery bill went up by, like, three hundred dollars and my electricity went up by a couple hundred as well. I know that you're still trying to figure stuff out, but in the meantime, do you think you could pitch in a bit for the bills?"

Blame it on your roommate/landlord, etc. If none of those options work for you, you could always blame the fact that you have to force them out on your roommate or your landlord, making that person the bad guy.

For example, "I'm totally fine having you here, but my roommate is a control freak and can't handle having someone on the couch. I'm really sorry, but I think it's time for you to find another couch. Do you think [insert a mutual friend's name here] would be okay with you staying there?"

A new friend goes on a rant about how lame plastic surgery is and how they wouldn't ever be friends with someone who would do that to themselves. You just put the down payment on your future fake boobs.

Well, your opinionated friend is going to figure out that some funny business is happening when your chest is suddenly twice as big, so you might as well let them know now.

★ **Awkward it up.** This is one of those situations where it's potentially entertaining to let the awkward train roll through, so if you decide to rock the boat a bit, you could follow up their proclamation with a smiling "So, does that mean you won't hang out with me anymore in two months once I have the boobs of my dreams?" Enjoy the open-mouthed stare and backpedaling.

To not be too much of a jerk after deliberately backing them into a corner, assure them that you totally get that people have differing personal opinions on plastic surgery and that you respect their opinion, but let them know you're completely excited about your future boobs, and you hope they'll support you as you would support them.

Something Awkward That (Might Have) Happened

>> THE MOVERS AND THE BOX O' DILDOS

My friend was moving and had invited some friends over the previous night to help him finish packing. The next day, as the movers (one of whom was his boss's brother) were loading the boxes on the moving truck, my friend noticed that one of his friends (or all of them—it was unclear) had relabeled the boxes with things like:

✱ Vibrators and Dildos: 12–18 Inches, Box 1 of 4
✱ Furry Porn, Titles *Another Squirrel in Paradise* to *(The) Fluffy Lion and I*
✱ Whips and Paddles, Box 1 of 10

The movers chuckled at some and raised eyebrows at others, and all avoided my friend's eyes. After a couple attempts to explain that his friends were responsible for the labeling, it was very clear from the "yeah, okays" and the "whatevers" that the movers (and especially his boss's brother) didn't believe him. Short of making a huge deal about it and diving into the boxes to prove that the whips and paddles were actually soccer gear, he didn't really have much recourse.

My friend did the only thing he could think of, which was to go with it. Clearly, denying the labels just made him look more freaky in their eyes (the lady doth protest too much, and all that), so he started egging them on, asking them if they wanted to see how impressive an eighteen-inch dildo looked. He figured the situation was so ridiculous that if there was any fallout from his boss learning about his "freaky sex life," he'd deal with it when it came up. Ultimately, weirding out the movers was way more fun than worrying about what his boss might think.

When the movers finished, one of them told my friend that he had won the "freakiest client we've ever had" award and slipped my friend his number as he left. Win.

When your lie meows . . .

(page 73)

2

Lying Fail

Lying successfully takes a lot of confidence and some planning to make sure we don't leave any obvious holes (which would lead to getting caught . . .).

Unfortunately, lying is rarely a planned event.

When we lie in our daily lives, 99 percent of the time we've given no forethought to our stories and are merely trying to avoid an awkward, uncomfortable, or embarrassing situation for ourselves or someone else. Since forethought is generally required to pull off a convincing lie, when we inevitably get caught lying, the awkwardness of the situation increases hundredfold, because now we're dealing with the original awkwardness (whatever it was we were afraid of dealing with in the first place) as well as looking like a bat-shit-crazy pathological liar. Escape plan fail.

So, whatever our reasons for telling a lie—telling one to protect ourselves, telling one to protect someone else, telling one to annoy someone else, telling one because it's easier than telling the truth, telling one for fun—and no matter what caused the awkwardness (e.g., getting caught lying or confronting someone else who lied), the Awkward Monster is going to be *rightthere* to keep us company. Avoiding the awkward can take many paths—some requiring a more enthusiastic leap to the dark side than others.

Behold the moral ambiguity.

 You told your girlfriend you were working late last night, and today your buddies show up at your house for the game and say, "Dude, that strip club was epic last night! I can't believe you were in the VIP room for three hours!" . . . in front of your girlfriend.

 Lie some more. Want to solve a lie with another lie and live in the relationship danger zone? If that's the case, try, "Guys—that wasn't me. That was Jeremy. Remember, you called me to go, but I had to work late? You guys must have been wasted last night!" If your friends are quick enough on the uptake to go along with it, it's *possible* you may weasel your way out of the lie, but more likely you'll be dealing with a very pissed significant other.

 Make a bad joke. Tell your friends thanks for reminding you, and then jokingly tell your girlfriend that you're dumping her for Candy, on whom you dropped several thousand dollars last night and who never complains or criticizes you, is always in excellent shape, and has fantastic breasts. Laugh because you were obviously—in your eyes—just making a joke to lighten the situation. Watch how no one else joins in. Watch your girlfriend leave.

Tell the truth: You like motorboating. Turn to your girlfriend, take her hands in yours, and say, "I'm really sorry for lying, but the reason I went to the strip club last night is because I like looking at—and getting lap dances from—attractive, naked women. It doesn't mean I love you any less." Smile.

★ **Confess and apologize.** Pull her aside, apologize to her for lying, and give her some reason why you lied—you were scared she wouldn't approve, you were scared she'd be jealous (when she has no reason to be), you just needed a night away and didn't want to explain where you were going—and then talk about it for a few minutes. Does she want to come with you next time? If she's freaking out, is it because you lied or because you went to a strip club?

In the future, invite her along. Many girls (way more than the general public appears to think) dig going to strip clubs, and your girlfriend might be one of them. And who knows, you may be able to turn your lies into a positive for your relationship.

Dodge the Awkward Monster

Don't lie again. Duh. And if you must, warn your friends to cover for you.

▶▶ Handling photographic lies: You just got caught (on camera) doing something you weren't supposed to be doing.

The advent of picture messaging and mobile photo-uploading has made it almost impossible to lie your way out of getting busted.

Let's say you're dating two chicks at the same time. If, despite your best efforts, you get caught photographically in a lie—for example, you told Kaitlin that you had to stay in and study, but pictures of you and Brianna at a party have ended up all over Facebook—denying it will make you look a) like an idiot and b) as though you think Kaitlin is an idiot. Now you're going to get dumped for being dumb and for being a liar. Fail.

Burn the bridge. Tell Kaitlin you're glad she found out about Brianna. You've been meaning to dump her.

Run away. Avoid both of them so you don't have to deal with the confrontation, up to and including screening all your calls and pretending you have mono so you don't have to go to class or leave your apartment.

★ **Talk it out.** The most solid course of action to alleviate the awkwardness (and death glares) is to apologize for lying, listen to Kaitlin's feelings on the subject, and talk out anything that needs discussion (like the fact you're dating two girls at once). Understand that any trust she had in you has been broken and that it will take time to build it up again, and make amends as best you can by promising (honestly) not to do it again.

Dodge the Awkward Monster

If you're going to be lying about your whereabouts or what you're doing around your Facebook-photo-happy paparazzi friends, you need to plan ahead to defend yourself against photographic evidence, i.e., make your peeps promise not to upload any incriminating pictures.

You're dating two (or more) girls at once, and as #1's date to her office holiday party, you see #2 and realize she works with #1.

Play on, unskilled playa.

Seeing as how you haven't yet figured out how to make your two-person bed fit three (or four or five . . .), you need to deal with this. There are a few different options here, depending on how honest you were previously.

>> SITUATION 1: You've lied and told each girl that you're exclusive with her. They've figured it out and are pissed.

Liar, liar, pants on fire. If you've expressly told either one (or both . . . or *all*?) that you're exclusive with her, prepare yourself for intense hell-fury. You lied, and now you're going to have to deal with the fallout.

★ **Explain.** It's unlikely you'll be able to avoid #2 over the entire course of the evening (thereby keeping your lies intact), so your best bet is to preemptively explain to your date, #1, that when you said "exclusive," you were using your made-up definition of the word, indicating you were free to date other people. Then do the stand-up thing: Apologize to her and offer to leave.

You could also:

 Run. Then call #3—after all, you're dressed up and ready to party, right?

 Run. Feign food poisoning and go home for the night.

 Pretend you don't know #2. Because ignoring #2 totally won't lead to an infinitely more awkward conversation later on.

 Lie. Pretend you never told either of them you were exclusive. Act mystified when they get angry.

 Propose the threesome you've been dreaming about. Good luck escaping without getting slapped when you bring this up to the two women who just found out you've been lying to them and who both thought they were the only one for you. Expect not to hear from #1 or #2 again.

>> **SITUATION 2A: You haven't determined the relationship with any of them, leaving you (technically) free to roam, and you see girl #2 before she sees you.**

If you've never *said* things are exclusive, things are a bit different. However, if you've led each girl to believe (inadvertently or not) that she's the only one in your life, then as soon as you see #2, the solid thing to do is to let #1 know that someone's there whom you've recently gone out with a few times (thereby stating, in no uncertain terms, that you are not exclusive with either of them), that you realize the situation is pretty awkward, and that if she'd like, you can leave.

If #1 has been under the impression that the two of you are exclusive, you'll have to deal with her misconceptions. If your explanation and defusing go well, she may get over it and the two of you can continue the night's plans. Just be prepared to deal with some glares or an awkward conversation with #2.

The best way to handle #2 is to excuse yourself to say hi to #2 and, without making a huge deal out of it, to explain that you're there as #1's date. The conversation will probably be uncomfortable, but ignoring #2 would probably be worse. Remember to stay focused on #1 (and not dance or hang out with #2, beyond the quick "this is the deal" conversation)—you're #1's date for the night, after all, and she deserves your full attention.

>> SITUATION 2B: You haven't determined the relationship with either of them, leaving you (technically) free to roam, but girl #2 finds and confronts you before you have a chance to explain anything to #1.

If #2 approaches you when you're standing with #1, remain friendly and calm. If #2 starts getting snippy, you'll need to excuse yourself and step aside to explain things to #1 (she is, after all, your date), following the protocol in Situation 2A.

Under no circumstances should you try to play it off like #2 is a "friend"—any idiot can see right through that. Your trying to cover it up is going to be far more worrisome to #1 than if you're just honest and admit that her coworker (#2) is one of the other girls you're dating. If #1 wants you to leave, do so.

>> SITUATION 2C: Girl #2 catches you at the bar by yourself and confronts you.

If #2 finds you by yourself at the bar, follow a plan similar to Situation 2A, but don't offer to leave—you're there as #1's guest, so she takes precedence over #2 (unless, of course, #2 threatens to do something crazy if you don't leave—then you should talk to #1, explain the situation, bail, and seriously reconsider the kinds of decisions you've been making that got you stuck with a crazy jealous bitch).

Your goal, overall, is to be respectful but honest and to acknowledge that, yes, this is an awkward situation, but it's not your intention to make anyone (more) uncomfortable.

>> SITUATION 3: Neither one of them seems to care.

Propose a threesome immediately. Opportunities like this don't come around every day.

Dodge the Awkward Monster

In the future, to avoid such encounters (and to avoid having your dating habits shoved down your throat), make sure you're honest about the fact you're dating other people as soon as possible so there's no possibility of confusion.

It's a sad fact that some people in today's dating world have missed the memo that says all's fair until the DTR (Determine The Relationship) talk and you're not exclusive until you talk about it. These memo-missers are likely to assume that you're exclusive from the moment you make out. The easiest way to avoid future awkwardness with such people is to be up front and make sure everyone's on the same page, *especially* when things have lasted more than a couple weeks.

> Most people respect honesty about such things, and while they may not be cool with it, they'll appreciate your saying something.

You lied and said you liked the holiday fruitcake your friend made for you a few years ago, and now she makes one for you every year. You hate it, and so, as you do every year, you threw it away. Unfortunately, you forgot to empty the trash before she came over, and she just found her creation in the garbage. Now she's staring at you with tears in her eyes.

Lie your way out. You could lie and say that you woke up and found mouse footprints on it, so you couldn't eat her delicious concoction and had to throw it away, which you're super bummed about. But then she might just make you another one and you'll be stuck again.

Tell the truth: You hate fruitcake. You could also use this opportunity as a less-than-ideal way of letting her know your true feelings on her holiday baking. However, your brutal honesty may not be well received (given how she found out), and it's quite possible you'll lose her as a friend, you giant liar.

★ **Tell a little lie and be a little honest.** Since she caught you being a jerk, a somewhat solid (although morally ambiguous) way out is a combination of both—honesty so that she doesn't make the cake again, and lies to protect her feelings. Explain that the reason the cake is in the trash is because you accidentally left it out and were worried it was now harboring a bacterial

65

kingdom. And although you love her yearly contributions to your waistline, you're trying to stay healthy, so why don't the two of you skip the baked goods exchange next year and just enjoy a fun night out together. It will be a mutual gift to each other and will preserve your health (as well as assuage your guilty conscience).

She may or may not believe you. However, because you suggested something that includes hanging out with her as an alternative, she'll see that you clearly still like her, which is ultimately what she'd worry about if you offered no other reason for trashing the fruit(cake) of her hard kitchen labors.

 You call in sick on a beautiful, warm, sunny day. Then as you pick up a case of beer while wearing a swimsuit on your way to the beach, you run into your coworker who's buying groceries during their lunch hour.

Getting caught in a lie is always awkward, but if you think fast, you may have some options.

★ **Continue the lie.** Tell your coworker it's laundry day (hence the swimsuit), and you're at the store to buy Gatorade and saltine crackers to help you get through a horrible bout of food poisoning. Do your best to look sick. Pretend you're buying the beer for your roommate, who was super insensitive about your delicate condition and asked you to do her/him this favor while you're steps away from food-poisoned death. Look pathetic.

Create a new lie to cover for your old lie. For example, pretend you're your own identical twin. Have fun making up a backstory for why the coworker hasn't ever heard of you before (you're a long-lost sibling, you were in jail for the last twenty years, etc.). As for why you recognized the coworker when you shouldn't have ever seen them before (since you, as your twin, don't work with them)? Tell them you and your twin show each other pictures of everyone in your lives and tell each other everything, and from all the good things your twin has told you, the coworker must be [insert their name here]—no one else could be more handsome/beautiful and dress so well. Perhaps insincere flattery (bonus points for actually meaning it) and a few minutes of solid kiss-ass will get you out of the danger zone, even if this little stunt makes them reevaluate your sanity (once they find out that you don't, in fact, have a twin). Of course, if they buy your big tall tale, you'll need to keep up the act for as long as you're in contact with them—effectively creating Mt. Everest out of a sand dune since you'll have to keep lying . . . and lying . . . and lying. Let's be honest: This will fall apart eventually, although the journey might be fun.

 Run. Or hide. Then pretend you don't know what they're talking about when they ask you about it at work the next day.

 Confess. Shout "Busted!" when you see them and, with a sheepish grin, tell them you'll owe them one if they don't rat you out. They might still rat you out, but let's be honest—who hasn't taken an impromptu personal day every now and again?

You go along with something you don't like doing (like riding a roller coaster) to impress your crush. Your friend (who doesn't realize your subterfuge) asks you post-ride why you did it and calls you out on your fear by saying, "Don't you hate roller coasters? You told me last week you'd rather chew off your own arm than ride one." Now your crush is looking at you like you're crazy.

Your crush, confused, asks why you said you love roller coasters when you don't. This leads you to an impressive attempt at the gold medal in the blush-Olympics and serious contemplation of friendicide. Your friend remains blissfully unaware of the awkwardness s/he's just caused.

Deny, deny, deny. "I never said I hate roller coasters. What are you talking about?" This throws your friend under the bus and makes them look crazy instead. If they insist? You both look crazy. This isn't a great move for friend relations, and it's not perfect as an escape plan, but if you don't want to admit you lied, this is a workable out.

You suddenly changed your mind. There's no law that says you can't readjust your view of roller coasters. Take advantage of this and claim a 180-opinion. "I totally love roller coasters now! They're super fun." Try not to look how you feel: like puking.

Confess the whole truth. Admitting you lied involves admitting why—namely, that you like your crush and wanted to impress them by being cool with what they wanted to do. This can go one of two ways: "OMG, I like you too!" or "Oh . . ." followed by an awkward silence. Yikes.

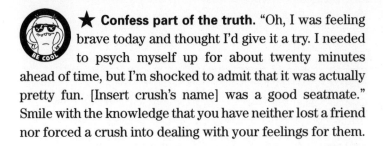 ★ **Confess part of the truth.** "Oh, I was feeling brave today and thought I'd give it a try. I needed to psych myself up for about twenty minutes ahead of time, but I'm shocked to admit that it was actually pretty fun. [Insert crush's name] was a good seatmate." Smile with the knowledge that you have neither lost a friend nor forced a crush into dealing with your feelings for them.

White lies: You lied about something small, like pretending you've had a shirt forever so that your date doesn't know you bought something new just to impress him/her. They just found the tag.

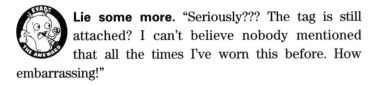 ★ **Confess.** With small lies like this, a confession (and an apology for lying) can be cute and endearing and can promote bonding. Pretty much everyone lies at some point, and with little stuff, it's typically not that big of a deal and shows vulnerability, which can be a good thing when we're engaged in the "I want you to like me but don't want to look like I'm trying too hard to make you like me" dating dance.

Lie some more. "Seriously??? The tag is still attached? I can't believe nobody mentioned that all the times I've worn this before. How embarrassing!"

Necessary lies: Someone catches you running away from them or pretending you didn't see them. Now they're confronting you about it.

Anyone who claims they've never run away, hidden, or ignored someone they didn't want to talk to (ever ducked behind a bush when your ex-boyfriend walked by? No?

That's just me?) is lying. Everyone does this at some point. It's never a conscious, well-thought-out plan, but rather a much more instinctual following of our body's fight-or-flight reaction to "Oh shit, it's them!"

And when we get caught? It's as if the Awkward Monster has bitch-slapped us.

 ★ **Offer an alternative explanation.** Put your keys on the ground, and then pretend you were looking for them to explain why you dove behind that parked car. Or be searching for a contact lens. Or tell them you thought you saw a quarter. Even if everyone involved knows that you were, in fact, hiding, your lie gives you plausible deniability and also gives the person something else to talk about besides your obvious rabbiting. This will help.

If you got caught running away, you can either a) claim you thought you were being chased by someone creepy or b) say you were chasing after someone who just stole something from the store you were in, and you wanted to play good Samaritan and help the store out.

★ **Confess.** This is super awkward and will make them regret asking. No one actually expects to hear, "Um, yep. I was hiding from/running away from/ignoring you." It will leave them speechless. Win.

▶▶ **You offered to do something for someone because you thought they'd say no. They just accepted, and now you have to take back your offer.**

Typically, people assume that if you're offering to do something for them, it's because you can *actually do that thing* and not that you're just pretending to offer only to rescind when they accept.

So, when you offer to drive your friend to their great-aunt's funeral, and you have neither a car nor a driver's license, you're going to look like a big jerk, and it's going to be really awkward.

To deal with this:

Step 1: Apologize. "I'm really sorry, but . . ."

Step 2: Look remorseful. This will indicate that you actually feel bad.

Step 3: "This is really awkward. . . ." (This will set the conversation up so that they're expecting something potentially negative or weird.)

Step 4: "Wow—do I ever feel like an asshole. . . ." (More remorse is good.)

Step 5: Once they've lost their patience with your stalling and are glaring at you, say:

> "Erm . . . um . . . Well, here's the deal. I can't actually drive you. I don't have a car or a license, and I only offered because I was sure you were going to say no and I wanted to make you feel like someone cared. So, I'm really sorry, but . . . yeah. I can't take you."

Step 6: Feel bad.

Step 7: Do your best to never again offer to do something you know you can't do.

★ **Lie to worm your way out of it.** Alternatively, and much less embarrassingly, you could pretend you remembered something you "already committed to" that you "can't get out of," so you're really sorry, but you can't take them after all. This is a widely used and somewhat socially acceptable excuse for getting yourself out of the "JK!" favor-lie.

You just got caught re-gifting.

Even if the thought behind the re-gift comes from the heart (you just *know* that the hand-knit orange sweater you got for Christmas last year would look better on your friend than on you), re-gifting is still awkward.

And if you break one of the rules of re-gifting in the process? You deserve every ounce of uncomfortable awkwardness coming to you.

Rule 1: Never re-gift a handmade or made-especially-for-you-gift.* Under no circumstances are you allowed to give a handmade-for-you gift to someone else for their birthday or for any other special occasion.

*The one exception to this rule is if you absolutely feel that the hand-knit orange sweater would be better on your friend than on you. Then, after a respectful period of time has elapsed since you received it (six months to a year), you may give it to your friend randomly as a Happy Thursday present and say, "I thought you might like this—I was going to give it to Goodwill because I realized a few days ago that orange looks awful with my new hair color, so if you don't like it, no biggie."

Rule 2: Never re-gift something used. Doing so is acceptable only if you know for a fact that your friend has been lusting after that thing for a long time (your old iPhone, for example). If this is the case, make a huge deal out of it and put the iPhone in a gigantic box with lots of layers of wrapping. This will make it fun and silly instead of serious. When re-gifting, fun and silly is much better than being genuinely excited and serious . . . especially when the re-gift receiver knows it's a re-gift.

Rule 3: Know the history of the gift. If you are going to re-gift, make sure you're not re-gifting something that was given to you by that person, or by anyone else who will see them opening it. This will result in questions like,

"Hey—isn't that the toaster I got you for your birthday last month?" This is awkward and there is no happy way out.

Something Awkward That (Might Have) Happened

>> THE DAY PUSSY GOT ME CAUGHT IN A LIE

I was living in an apartment that expressly forbade animals, but my friend Molly desperately needed a cat-sitter for the weekend, and since her house was waaaay out of my way, I agreed to let the cat stay with me for three days. I mean, what were the odds that the landlord would find out I had a stowaway just for a weekend? He was supposed to be out of town on a Hawaiian vacation that weekend anyway (something I knew because I was going to be collecting his mail for him).

Two weeks later when the appointed weekend arrived, Molly dropped off Pussy (the cat—yes, she named her cat Pussy, probably just so she could run around and yell "Pussy!"), and off she went on her weekend trip. I let Pussy out of her cage (ha!), and she immediately began roaming the apartment, meowing loudly. Thinking this was just a phase and that she would calm down after a few minutes, I let her do her thing.

Over the next seventy-two hours, the meowing stopped only for ten-minute increments every few hours.

The cat also:

✱ Sat between the curtains and the outside window, squished up against the glass and in full view of everyone who walked by my apartment (which was everyone in the building, because I was one apartment away from the entrance)—not an ideal situation when you're claiming you don't have a cat. Despite my duct-taping the shades to the surrounding walls so she couldn't get to the window, she still managed to find a hole and resume her highly visible, fur-squished-against-the-glass post.

* Found every possible hiding spot in my apartment, giving me several heart attacks as I thought I'd lost her, and forcing me to walk around yelling "Pussy!" at the top of my lungs. (Damn you, Molly!) I still wonder what my neighbors thought I was really doing.

* Almost got me kicked out of my rent-controlled apartment.

On the third day, a few hours before Molly was due to return to pick up her bundle of fluff, I heard a knock at my front door. Looking around for the cat (she was under my bed in the next room and being blissfully quiet), I shut the door to that room and made sure there weren't any other visible signs of her (litter box, food bowls, hacked-up hair balls, vomit, etc.), then opened the door. My landlord, who was miraculously back early from his vacation, was standing outside, looking harassed. He sighed and said, "You know you're not allowed to have animals in the apartment, right?"

I ignored his question. "Hey! Aren't you supposed to be in Hawaii?"

"Yeah. I am. [*Another sigh.*] You do know about the animal rule, right?"

"Um, yeah. Yes. I know that."

"Okay. So why is it that 3B told me you have a cat?"

"A cat? I don't have a cat." (Technically, this was true, since I was just cat-sitting for the weekend. . . .)

"Why would she say you have a cat if you don't have a cat? That makes no sense."

"I have no idea. I was watching some nature show last night—maybe that was it. But I can assure you I don't own a cat." [*Emphasis on "own."*]

"All right. Sorry to bother you. I just have to follow up—"

From behind me: "MEEEEEOOOOOOWWWWW. MEEEEEEEEEEEEOOOOOW. MEEEEEOW!"

My landlord paused, raised a skeptical eyebrow, and stared at me. "I . . . I just . . . [*Pause.*] I have to follow up with all complaints. [*Cough.*] That sure sounded like a cat."

I swallowed nervously. "Yeah, it sure did. Weird, right?"

As I ~~lied~~ talked, he suddenly shifted his focus from my face to the floor behind me. I turned around, and there was the cat, miraculously free from behind the shut door of the bedroom and sitting quietly three feet behind me, staring up at us and twitching her tail.

I sighed. He sighed. I avoided his stare for a very long and awkward pause and blushed furiously. He rubbed his face with his hand and looked even more harassed. Pussy, who probably noticed the tension, meowed loudly again.

Me: "I can explain. . . ."

I didn't end up getting kicked out, but I did have to pay a $250 "pet deposit" in case Pussy had dirtied anything while rooming with me. Molly only paid me $100.

*&%.

When you accidentally sext message your boss instead of your boyfriend . . .

(page 79)

Sexual, Dating, and Romantic Mishaps

When sex, dating, and romance take a turn for the worse, things get weird, uncomfortable, and really, really, really, *really* awkward, really fast.

When we're naked (or we plan to be) with someone we like (especially when they're a new someone we like), insecurities have a tendency to come bolting out of the holes they usually hide in, with bells on, ready to join the party. Egos get involved, and the probability of inadvertently insulting our partner goes way up. Fear, expectations, and excitement also join in the orgy, resulting in epic potential for insane amounts of OMFG awkwardness. Nip slips at work, getting caught masturbating, and first-date hell—all are covered here.

▶▶ **After one too many glasses of pinot at the office holiday party, you grabbed your coworker's ass on a dare, something that your sober self would have never done. Now things are weird.**

Unfortunately, this one gets super awkward really fast because it probably falls under the sexual-harassment umbrella, putting you in a heap of trouble if anyone decides to get offended. Your best bet is to apologize profusely and assure your coworker it won't happen again.

Apologize. Don't make excuses (like telling them that they "totally looked like they wanted you to") or mention the dare—it can really suck finding out you were the idiot picked out of the crowd to be the subject of a dare, especially if it involves something sexual. Were you picked because they thought you wouldn't get mad? Because you would? Because you're ugly? Because the group finds you attractive? Help them avoid the internal deluge of questions by just keeping the dare part to yourself.

Stick to the apology and leave it at that.

If they say, "No apology necessary—let's do this," and start acting like you're dating (and that's not what you want), welcome to your self-made hell, you ass-grabbing monkey, you. You started this, so you'll have to deal with it. Your best course of action is to shut it down, immediately.

This will be awkward because, effectively, you've led them on, but it's necessary unless you want to keep digging your hole. Use one of the following to get out of this:

 ★ **Blame it on work.** Explain that although your actions spoke otherwise, you acted in a moment of weakness and have since realized that an at-work relationship isn't smart. Act tortured by your decision, but make it clear that your mind is made up and this thing between you isn't going to happen.

Tell the truth. Tell them you're sorry, but your handsy moment was the result of a dare and you don't like them that way. Expect both hurt feelings and a potential sexual harassment suit.*

"Whoops!" Tell them you thought they were someone else, and you're really sorry, but the cupping of their (admittedly firm and pleasing) cheek wasn't meant for them.

"It was a compliment." Tell them you're sorry for the mix-up, but you couldn't help yourself that night—their buns just looked too good. Then explain that you do this to every great ass you see and it's nothing personal, nor does it mean anything—you were just being complimentary. Expect a sexual harassment suit.*

You just sent a suggestive text. It was meant for your significant other. You accidentally sent it to your boss.

Something Awkward That (Might Have) Happened

My friend was the executive assistant to the CFO of her company, and on a business trip, she accidentally sent a picture of her boobs to her boss instead of her boyfriend. The CFO, who was also on the business trip, received the picture and took it as an invitation.

A few minutes later (when she was wearing clothes again), she heard a knock at her door. As she hadn't yet

---

*BTW, I'm not a lawyer—but I'm pretty sure you'd lose.

realized her mistake, she thought her boss just wanted to review his schedule for the next day, so she was very surprised to find him wearing only a bathrobe. Brushing it off as a weird-but-whatever moment, she let him in and turned around to grab her BlackBerry and files to prepare for whatever he wanted to review. When she turned back around, she found her fifty-five-year-old boss standing in front of her wearing only his plaid boxers and his socks. As she tells it, the conversation that followed went something like this:

Her, *with an openmouthed stare*: ". . ."

Him, *smiling*: "I got your picture. This is definitely against HR policy, but I'm game if you are. No one has to know."

Her, *still not getting what happened*: "Um . . . what picture? What are you talking about?"

Him, *now staring at her boobs*: "The picture you sent me of your breasts. I'll admit it was kind of a shock at first, but my divorce is final next month, and like I said— no one has to know."

Her, *realizing what happened and covering her face with her hands*: "Oh my god. Ohmygod. That wasn't supposed to go to you—it was supposed to go to my boyfriend. OHMYGOD. This is so embarrassing!! I'm so sorry. OhmyGOD!!"

Him, *picking up his robe and putting it on*: "Oh, I see. Um, well then . . . this is most inappropriate. I apologize. I think it would be best if we agreed not to speak of this to anyone, don't you?"

Her, *blushing furiously*: "Oh god. Um, yes—yeah. I won't say anything . . . ever. Ohmygod. I'm so sorry! I'm so so so so sosososososo sorry. This is so awkward and embarrassing and ohmygod. This can't be happening. . . ."

Him, *noticing her discomfort and, presumably in an attempt to make her feel better, patting her on the shoulder*: "Well, dear, I won't argue with you that it's awkward, but you shouldn't be embarrassed. Since we're well past the point of propriety, I feel I can say this—you've got the best pair of tits I've seen in a long time. Your boyfriend is a lucky man." He then smiled, turned around, and left, shutting the door behind him.

Apparently, their working relationship was even better after this incident and not weird at all. She said that he was pretty stand-up about the whole thing, treating her only with respect and kindness. Once she got over feeling awkward around him, she felt a level of camaraderie that wasn't there before, and now their completely platonic relationship is one of her favorites.

This anecdote does not serve as any sort of recommendation to sext your boss, but I think it's worth noting that the epitome of awkward doesn't always have to end badly. Going through something so uncomfortable with another person can serve as a bonding session and have unexpected positive outcomes . . . like gaining an ally for life in your boss.

Even if the situation doesn't escalate to the level of your boss offering him- or herself to you, you've still got to deal with it. Approaching your boss as soon as possible after the pictures have arrived in their full glory is recommended, as is the most heartfelt apology you've ever mustered. You've put your boss in an extremely awkward position (think about what it would be like if you got similar pictures from them), and even though it's possible they will get that it was an honest mistake, there are legal ramifications* for sexual innuendoes and suggestive pictures sent in the workplace, whether they were intentional or not.

....
* Again, I'm not a lawyer, so I can't speak to specifics, but I'm pretty sure they're the bad kind of ramifications.

And if you used your work phone to take and send the pictures . . . Really? Was that really the best idea?

Dodge the Awkward Monster

First off, next time triple-check the "To" before you sext. Duh.

▶▶ **You're talking to your friend Joe at a crowded party about a recent sexual conquest. Just as you're relating how you were "pounding her like a jackhammer," everyone else's conversations experience a lull, and your descriptions are heard far and wide.**

 ★ **Escalate the awkwardness until it's funny.** Pretend you don't notice the silence and continue talking, using the most ridiculous adjectives you can think of to describe your encounter. Exaggerate. Elaborate more than necessary. Use large hand and body gestures to reenact what you did. People will laugh. It will be funny.

Go with it. Smile, wave at the smiles around you to acknowledge that you know they're listening, and continue talking to Joe. This shows confidence, and you never know who may be listening and will want to be your next conquest after hearing about your "skillz."

Laugh it off. Grin sheepishly and allow your red cheeks and ears to show themselves. Then say something like "That was awkward," to the general vicinity and have a good laugh with Joe as you wait for the conversations around you to resume.

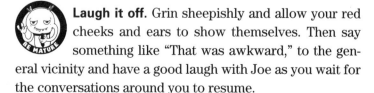

You stretch your arms while wearing a tight button-up shirt at work and the button(s) pop off, exposing your bra and causing you to have a nip slip in front of your boss.

 Don't freak out. The best way to handle this one is to stay calm, apologize profusely, and excuse yourself to fix your shirt and/or put something on over it to prevent any further nipple flashes.

If you notice the draft after the fact, you could bring it up to your boss and apologize, but honestly, this may unnecessarily prolong an already uncomfortable situation. Your boss is surely aware that you didn't mean to flash your goods, so you don't have to apologize for anything deliberate. As long as you fix your shirt and make sure that the girls are modestly tucked in for work in the future, there's no real need to bring it up.

The dos and don'ts of starting a conversation (with someone you like).

This is one topic I'm very well versed in: My previous book* details my many years of disastrous attempts at starting conversations with guys, all in the name of figuring out how to talk to someone you like without having to hand your gift-wrapped ego to them.

Whether you call it a pickup line or just talking, starting a conversation with someone you find sexy is filled with

---

* My first book is a dating guide for women about how to talk to and meet men (although, as it turns out, many guys found it useful as a guide for how to meet women as well). It's called *Screw Cupid: The Sassy Girl's Guide to Picking Up Hot Guys* (The Experiment, 2009). For more info, check out www.samanthascholfield.com.

potential awkward land mines. Overarching all interactions of this nature is the universal fear of getting rejected, which causes all manner of awkwardness: shifty eyes, squeaky voice, nervous sweating, stuttering, etc.

Something Awkward That (Might Have) Happened

>> PICKUP LINE FAIL

To give you some background: I was in the midst of testing out my theory that if guys used pickup lines like "It's okay if you buy me a drink . . . and nice ass," and were successful doing so, then it might work in the opposite direction as well. I was just coming off a successful attempt at initiating conversation with a guy I liked when the following occurred, and so was somewhat delusional in my thinking that one success meant I knew what I was doing.

My friends and I were out barhopping, and in the interest of testing out my pickup line theories, I picked out a guy who easily would have earned a unanimous rating of 9.5 from a female audience. He was sitting at the bar with two of his guy friends, his back facing me. I wasn't too nervous—I mean, what was the worst that could happen? He'd say no? I could handle that.

I walked over to the 9.5 and leaned against the bar next to him, casually (or so I thought) letting my padded bra brush his back in what I hoped was a sexy move. However, I must have misjudged how much padding I had attached to my chest, because when I slid in next to him, I ended up pushing him off his chair. It wasn't such a push that he fell out of his chair, but it did quite nicely manage to make him lose his balance and spill about half his drink on the floor. This was unfortunate for me because there wasn't anyone on my other side who could be used as an excuse for why I had gotten so close to him. In fact, when I glanced frantically in that direction to see what I could use as an excuse, I noticed there were two empty stools on my other side.

The 9.5 whirled around, noticed the enormous gap of air to my right, and to my mortification, instead of greeting me with the "hey baby" I'd expected (boob mishap aside), he said, "What the fuck. God," and turned back around to his friends.

Although I found the 9.5's reaction to be a bit extreme, I decided to forge ahead anyway and test out the infamous line: "It's okay if you buy me a drink . . . and nice ass." I repeated the magical phrase to the 9.5 and got no response from him at all. He didn't even turn around. Figuring he hadn't heard me, I said it louder: "IT'S OKAY IF YOU BUY ME A DRINK—AND NICE ASS." Once again, I had underestimated my strength and ended up bellowing at him instead of merely getting his attention. I also caught the attention of everyone within ten feet of us, all of whom stopped talking to look at me.

The 9.5, who had shrugged his shoulders up against his ears during my bellow, turned around and said—excuse me, shouted—"I HEARD YOU THE FIRST TIME." As he turned back to his laughing friends, I observed that his face had contorted into a look that fell squarely in the camps of both extreme annoyance and utter disgust. It finally sank in that a) amazingly, the line hadn't worked—in fact, it had gotten me the opposite of the reaction I'd been so sure I would get—and b) I'd probably never be able to show my face in that bar again. I don't know how I managed to exit the premises without further humiliation, but somehow I managed it. To this day, I still blush in deep embarrassment whenever I think of that moment. It rated an easy 15 on an awkwardness scale of 1 to 10 and was the single most mortifying experience of my life.

In the interest of helping us all get through our introductory "I don't know you but I think you're cute" conversations with as little awkwardness as possible, here are some handy guidelines I've gathered from my epic dating disasters:

Know what you want to say before you say it. The ability to come up with something to say on the fly is a rare skill, and the person who can do this well is even more rare. For the rest of us, knowing roughly what we want to say before we actually speak is generally a good idea. Stumbling over our words, squeaking because our voice cracks, and falling prey to those awful, awful awkward silences that can bombard the opening minutes of a pickup attempt are obviously things we all want to avoid.

Don't make it obvious that you want their number and/or to get in their pants. To guarantee that a pickup attempt will become awkward, announce to the object of your affection that you find them sexy, with a line such as "I don't say this very often, but I think you're beautiful." This will make them very uncomfortable and make the whole interaction extremely awkward-pause-ridden while they frantically search for something to say after "Thanks" and try to assess whether or not you're a serial killer.

While canned and unoriginal compliments (e.g., "I think you're beautiful") may be appreciated, they rarely start a conversation that goes where you want it to (e.g., a date or headlong into bed). This is because it's far less interesting to know immediately how someone feels about you. You'd much rather see that a person has some dignity and confidence and learn some interesting things about them so that, when the mutual flirting commences, it feels as though you're both deciding to like each other at that time. When the object of your attention knows you want them, it makes for some very uneven and unequal "getting to know you" terrain, on which they have the advantage. Equal ground is much better, far sexier, and way more fun.

86

Don't be an overly cocky douche or a timid rabbit. Another good way to make things awkward is to be overly confident to the point of smarmy jerkdom or, on the opposite end, overly shy to the point of stuttering, speaking too quietly, not making eye contact, not standing up straight, shuffling your feet, or wringing your hands.

Sitting right in the middle—confident, humble, and happy—is the very best place to be, and will almost guarantee a non-awkward interaction with the person you're trying to catch.

Do embrace awkward silences. Making fun of and acknowledging that there's an awkward silence or that a joke fell flat is a great way to break the tension and push something that's not going that well into more positive territory. This shows a level of confidence one doesn't very often find—being able to laugh at yourself and your failed jokes is hot.

Then again, if it's really not going well (because you've missed the subtle signals that they're so not into you), acknowledging the awkwardness is likely to make things more awkward. If they unsmilingly reply in a deadpan, I-couldn't-be-less-interested-in-you voice, "Yeah—it is awkward," and then look at anything but you, the good news is that at least then you'll know, in no uncertain terms, how they feel, and you can bail. So really, acknowledging the awkwardness is a win-win.

Don't wig out when you get rejected. Getting rejected sucks, no matter how long you've known the person. When dealing with first-date or first-encounter rejections, it's easy to make things really uncomfortable. For example, crying hysterically, getting angry, hurling insults, and/or making a scene in any way are all good ways to escalate the awkwardness.

To avoid this, ideally a first-encounter rejection should be handled by the dumpee with a smile and much indifference. This will confuse the dumper and make them wonder what they just lost. An "Oh, okay. Enjoy your night. Bye!" (plus a smile) is perfect.

A first-date rejection, although slightly harder to deal with, should be handled with respect for your date's feelings about the situation and with your emotions as reined in as possible. Something like "You've clearly thought about this, so if that's how you feel, I guess that's it" is great.

Again, this show of confidence and indifference will confuse the dumper and make you look like the cool one. Keep this up after the fact by not contacting them romantically and, if you do run into them, by being friendly. Making continued (and let's be honest, increasingly pathetic) attempts to see them and/or spark their interest in you will not only erase any cool points you earned for your initially confident reaction, but also add many, many points to your crazy meter. (I speak from personal experience on the pathetic/crazy front. . . .)

On the other hand, making a big scene, while awkward because you'll look like a crazy person, has the perk of embarrassing the hell out of the dumper in front of everyone else and could be a great way to get back at them. It's up to you.

 You're midway through a first or second date and realize that there's not a shot in hell of this working.

The best reaction to this depends first on how you're feeling about the person, and secondly on how they're feeling about you.

Dodge the Awkward Monster

When you're not sure how you feel about a first or second date going in, schedule an activity that has a natural ending after thirty minutes to an hour—giving you an out should you need one. Do not ever agree to something requiring a commitment of more time than you can handle should you realize that you hate the person.

>> SITUATION 1: You'd rather frolic naked in a refrigerator box full of spiders than spend one more second with your date. If they've said or done something that bugs you to the point where looking them in the eyes is a challenge, being honest and ending it then will do you both a favor—you won't waste your time and they won't waste theirs. To leave, you can try any of the following, which show various levels of respect for your date:

 ★ **Be nice.** "Hey, I'm just not feeling a connection and am not seeing this going anywhere, so I'm going to head out. Thanks for the [coffee/drink/burrito—whatever you're bailing on], and have a good day."

 Be not so nice. "Satan just called, and he wants you back in hell, stat. Have a great life."

 Be honest. "Wow—you're a crazy bitch. Peace."

>> SITUATION 2: There's no spark, but they're not evil. If you realize it will never work romantically, but you're having an okay time, let the date end naturally and just don't call them again. Chances are good that if you're not feeling it, neither are they, so your mutual dissatisfaction will work out well.

If they say "See you soon" or "Let's do this again," you could be honest and mature and say "So, I think I need to be honest here—I think you're cool, but I'm not feeling a romantic spark, so while it could be fun to hang out again, it would be as friends. I just don't want to give you the wrong impression. I hate it when people do that." Alternatively,

89

you could give a noncommittal response like "Yeah, maybe" or "Yeah, see you around," and then just not return their calls, thereby assuring the continued success of the "Why didn't s/he call?" dating advice industry.

>> SITUATION 3: You can tell they're already planning the wedding. If you're not into it, but they're obviously into you, do the right thing and let them know what's up at the end of the date (or bail early if you're getting "I'm obsessed with you" vibes). Something like:

> "Hey, thanks for meeting up with me today. Although [you're really nice/I've had a fun time/I've enjoyed your company], I'm just not feeling a romantic spark, so I'm going to head out."

This will save them many agonizing hours wondering whether or not you'll call them (or call them back), and then even more hours wondering why you didn't call them: After all, the date (from their perspective) was awesome.

Dodge the Awkward Monster

WHEN THINGS GET REALLY AWKWARD
If, when you let them know you're just not that into them, they start hysterically crying or otherwise freaking out, you have a few different options:

1. **Bail anyway. As harsh as it sounds, you may have been the trigger for their freak-out, but it's not your responsibility to help them through it.**
2. **★ Grab a napkin for their tears, apologize, and bail. A slightly more compassionate version of just bailing; you still recognize that this is their deal, not yours.**

3. Join in on the freak-out. Misery loves company, so really, you're just being nice.

4. Tell them you were just kidding and stick around for another four hours to avoid hurting their feelings. Because the type of person who cries in public upon being respectfully rejected after a fifteen-minute date is totally stable and will definitely not wig when they find out you've been lying about liking them.

Finally, some of the best stories for your friends come from truly awful dates. If you have time to kill, embrace your date's awkwardness and/or douchebaggery/bitchiness and see if you can goad them into doing something truly horrible.

Everyone loves a good bad-date story, and your sacrifice will add many minutes of material to your funny-story box. Next time you're in need, like at a cocktail party when you're trying to make everyone laugh (especially that cute guy/girl in the corner), it will be ready for you to pull out.

Something Awkward That (Might Have) Happened

>> DATES GONE AWKWARD

Let me tell you a little story about this dude I went on a date with once:

I found him on a dating site. I can't remember who emailed whom first, but the email exchanges were good. We set up a date at a local wine bar, and at first glance, everything was great. He was the same guy as in his profile picture (which was nice), and the picture was obviously recent, since he matched it. Win. He had tattoos (I was into this at the time) and otherwise looked good. We bought drinks and sat down in the corner of the bar to chat.

91

To set the scene, the bar was pretty empty—we were in the corner, and two other couples were sitting about five feet away on either side of us. It was pretty quiet, so we could all easily hear each other's conversations. About ten minutes into our conversation, I was actually starting to consider that we might have second-date potential. He was funny and smart and seemed cool . . .

. . . at least until things got weird fast:

"So . . . I should warn you about something."

Oh shit, I thought. *What is it this time? Some new, virulent STD? Married with ten kids? There's a price on his head from a gambling debt?* "Um . . . okay. What's up?"

[*Leaning back, spreading his legs slightly, with a smirk.*] "I've had complaints."

What the F was he talking about? "I don't get it. Complaints about what . . . ?"

[*Pointing to his crotch.*] "This. My cock is huge."

At this point, I glanced around to see if anyone else had heard him. . . . Surely I had made it up? I mean, who says that? However, it quickly became clear that both of the other couples had heard this announcement, since they were now snickering behind their hands and leaning in to better hear what my date was saying. I looked back at my date, who apparently hadn't noticed that I'd looked away or that he had an audience, as he was still talking.

". . . it's absolutely huge. Most girls complain about how much it hurts. I mean, I feel bad about that, but if they can't deal with the power—that's their problem, right? It seems like we're heading in that direction, so it seemed only fair to warn you ahead of time. . . ."

Finally, it dawned on me that he was serious, and that he was completely unaware of the laughter (things had graduated from snickering) coming from both couples on either side of us. As I watched in WTF-is-going-on mode, he repeatedly gestured to his crotch and pointed to a spot about two-thirds of the way down his thigh, which presumably was his length measurement at full capacity.

I alternated between being horrified and amused as I tried to figure out a nice way to get out of the conversation and leave without being a complete bitch. I mean, he was so sincere—maybe he actually felt like he was doing me a favor by warning me?

However, after he talked for twenty minutes straight without looking up from his crotch, I interrupted, and I think I said something about how I forgot to wash my cat so I could bail. My bitch-filter was sufficiently clogged after his much-too-lengthy penis-centric filibuster. Anyone that obsessed with his manhood and himself deserved any bitchiness coming to him.

This particular situation actually would have been even *more* awkward had he not spent quite so much time talking about his dick and expected some kind of response from me about his warning. Thank the dating gods for small favors.

Attack of the first-date killer: The awkward pause.

We've all been there. The conversation seems to be rolling along nicely—recent news, the weather, and what you do for work have all been discussed in detail. And then the dreaded pause sets in.

"So . . ."

"So."

"So, do you have any pets?"

"Nope. Do you?"

"I had a dog when I was kid. He died."

93

"Oh. I'm sorry."

"Yeah. It was a long time ago."

" . . . "

" . . . "

"So . . ."

You stare at the ceiling, the floor. You stir your drink, you take a sip of your drink, you watch the other people in the bar—all the while frantically trying to come up with something, *anything* to talk about so that this awful awkwardness will end.

Here's a handy list of conversation starters to keep on hand. (You might even go so far as to write them down in your phone or on a piece of paper in your bag, for easy reference whenever the Awkward Monster sneaks up and sits on your face.)

* What's the worst date they've ever been on? (*Note:* Do not ask what the best date was. This is awkward because it means that they'll obviously have to think about the person they went on the awesome date with, and not you. And once they realize that's what they're doing and they can tell you know, it will be awkward. Don't go there.)

* If they could live in any country in the world, what country would it be and why?

* What's their worst/favorite vacation story? (To avoid the obvious awkwardness of talking about exes, decide ahead of time that you'll both refer to any vacation that involved an ex as one you went on by yourself.)

* Where have they traveled and what's the craziest story to come out of those travels?

* What was their most embarrassing moment in high school? College? Since then?

* What's their dream job?

✱ What's their dream life look like? (Make sure to couch this not as an interrogatory and judgmental "Is their career path and life plan reasonable?" question, but rather an easygoing question meant to ferret out wildest dreams about writing a book, owning a B&B in Costa Rica, going on safari in Africa, or sailing around the world. Very interesting conversation can come out of this because it's often easier to talk about your crazy dreams with a stranger rather than with someone who knows you well.)

✱ Do they like Almond Joy? (Seriously—I've never met anyone who has answered that in the affirmative.)

✱ Top five favorite movies, by genre if necessary, and/or the last movie they saw.

✱ Top five favorite books or the last book they read.

✱ Top five favorite bands and/or albums and/or what's on their current favorite playlist.

✱ What magazines do they read cover-to-cover every month?

✱ Best concert they've ever gone to.

✱ Craziest thing they've ever tried (think food) or done (wrangling rattlesnakes).

✱ What's their personal description of hell? (Mine involves parrots, large public restrooms, clowns with knives, pill-bottle cotton, and lots of mangoes—see? Weird. Don't you want to know more?)

✱ Make up backstories about the people around you.

✱ Ask them if they've seen your favorite humorous websites, and if they haven't, show them examples of the best posts on your smartphone.

✱ Ask random questions like: Why are moths perceived as so universally creepy and butterflies aren't?

If you get caught with your conversation-starter list, admit it. It will be endearing because you're being vulnerable by admitting you brought a list. Also, it's flattering. You wouldn't have made the list if you weren't nervous, and you wouldn't be nervous if you didn't like this person. Win-win.

▶▶ **You go on a date with someone new and end up back at their place. At that point, you realize that their new roommate is your ex, whom you dated for four months over a year ago.**

Make it worse. The fun option here is to not mention that you dated the roommate, hook up with the new person, and then scream the roommate's name during the height of passion. This is a great way to a) let your ex know that you're not over them (or that you are and are taunting them), and b) let the new person know about your history with their roommate.

★ **Admit the connection.** If you're not feeling douchey, it's best to deal with this head-on and tell the new person as soon as you have a chance that you and their roommate have history. Leaving a secret like this to be unearthed when you run into your ex in your date's kitchen the next morning is not likely to end well. Also, for the sake of everyone's feelings and selfishly avoiding those super-awkward potential run-ins with your ex, schedule all trysts for your place instead of theirs.

▶▶ **You hit on someone in a public place (like a coffee shop), and it goes badly—in front of an audience.**

Let's say you, in a solid attempt to start a conversation, say something to the rejecter like "Hey—sorry to bug you, but I couldn't help but notice you're using the new Kindle. How do you like it? I'm thinking about getting one." And they

96

reply (more loudly—and way more bitchily—than neces-sary) with, "No, I don't want to fuck you."

Everyone watching knows exactly how embarrassed you are, because they've all been there, too, which makes this extra awkward because it's hard to convincingly play it like you're not embarrassed.

Your options are:

Give them an "are you crazy?" look and reply with, "Who said anything about sex?" Then walk away. A defensive reaction, but effective, as it will make them look crazy and take the focus off you (because everyone will look at them to see their reaction), which is good. This way you can blush in embarrassment at such epic public failure in semi-privacy.

Swallow audibly, look at your feet, and shuffle away. You're embarrassed and everyone knows it. This will make you look like a doormat but may garner you sympathy from the crowd, which isn't necessarily a bad thing.

★ **Say with a sarcastic smile, "Wow—you're super nice . . ." and exit, head held high.** It's confident, and it calls them out on their rudeness, which is good. You'll earn respect and sympathy from the peanut gallery, all at once. Yay.

Say, "You should be so lucky." This will make you look like a total ass, but if your rejecter is into it, it could end well.

97

You just ran into the guy/girl you went out with last month on a date (that you thought sucked). They've called you four times since then asking to hang out, so apparently your not-so-subtle radio silence isn't working.

Since you're the one who's acted like a jerk by not setting set the record straight after the third phone call (when it became clear they weren't picking up on your subtle silence), your options are as follows:

 Act happy to see them. Want to see what suspicious glares look like? You'll get one if you act exactly the opposite of the way they were expecting. When they ask why you haven't called them back, you can a) act like you don't know what they're talking about ("What calls?"); b) wuss out and tell them you've just been really busy and haven't been returning anyone's calls (and prepare yourself to receive more calls); or c) be a jerk and tell them you're glad you ran into them because you're really confused as to why they've been calling you—wasn't it obvious there was no chemistry on the date you had? Expect hurt feelings.

Run away. This will provide all but the most persistent with the crystal-clear message that you're a) not interested and b) a giant wuss.

★ **Acknowledge the awkwardness and 'fess up.** When presented with the cold, hard truth (i.e., you weren't into seeing them again romantically but didn't have the guts to tell them that) and an apology for not being more stand-up about it, most people will respect your opinion and the air will clear.

Something Awkward
That (Might Have) Happened

>> AWKWARD OPINIONS ON DATES

One particularly rambunctious Saturday, I was out with a few friends, one of whom had brought a girl he'd recently met (it was their first date) to hang out with us for the evening.

Toward the end of the evening, as things were winding down, we found a low-key bar and were in one of the booths enjoying a conversation about music, when a (super-annoying) popular song started playing that we immediately all started talking about. There were five of us at that point—me, my two friends, this guy (we'll call him Tom), and his date (we'll call her Kelly). The conversation that ensued was one of the more awkward ones I've witnessed.

Friend 1: "God! I hate this song! Why do they have to play it so much?"

Friend 2: "I have no idea. It sucks."

Me: "Yeah. It sounds like they're talking about gonorrhea instead of love."

Tom, *laughing*: "Totally! Like, if the STD Council of America needed a theme song, this should be it."

Friend 1, *laughing*: "Or the Greek system."

Friend 2, *laughing*: "Ha! Maybe that's what they were secretly going for—maybe it's a message to the youth of America to wear condoms so it doesn't burn when they 'love.'"

During all of this, Tom's date, Kelly (who hadn't said more than fifteen words the whole night), finally looked like she might want to join in. After a thirty-second pause where no one said anything and (at least I know I thought) the conversation had moved on, she spoke up:

"This is my favorite song, and it's not about STDs. It's about love. It's my ringtone, and I listen to it on repeat before I go to sleep every night. I'm going to their concert next week."

None of us knew how to respond. She delivered her statements with such sincerity and was so obviously offended by what we'd said, we were at a loss for what to say to make it better, if anything. Tom looked at each of us in desperation, and then looked at her and gave her this sort of half-smile face that I think was trying to both look sympathetic and ask for forgiveness, but ended up coming across as kind of a creepy leer.

Kelly: ". . ."

More awkward silence.

My two friends and I were doing our best to look everywhere but at them, so as not to get sucked into the awkward tension that was sizzling on the other side of the booth. Tom clearly liked Kelly, but he had just stumbled into one of the most awkward of first-date potholes—the severely differing opinion. First dates are about bonding, and bonding happens faster when we figure out we have the same opinions and likes/dislikes as others. Sure, having wildly different tastes in music isn't a deal breaker, but considering this was the first thing Kelly had said besides "Yes, I'd like a drink" all night, the awkwardness was palpable.

Tom, *to us, swallowing audibly and obviously extremely uncomfortable*: "So . . . you guys going to the party next week?"

You recently hit on someone you see frequently, even everyday (like the barista, your bank teller, the UPS delivery guy, or the receptionist at your dentist's office), but they said no. Now it's awkward every time you see them . . . which is a lot.

Keep trying. Maybe pestering them will wear them down. Also, if you act like you're joking (or actually joke about it) by saying any of the following each time you see them—"Ready to say yes yet?" "How about today?" and "Single yet?"—with a smile, it's possible they'll find it entertaining and it can be a joke between the two of you. If they take it well, this can be a great way to alleviate the awkwardness and show that you're not too bothered by their rejection.

However, if they don't take it well and feel sexually harassed, you can count on things getting infinitely more awkward when you get asked to frequent another coffee shop, dentist's office, or bank and suddenly have a new UPS guy on your route.

Escalate it to the point where they say yes just to alleviate the awkwardness. Every time you see them, make a show of acting embarrassed and super nervous, especially if you were carefree, chatty, and lighthearted around them before. Say things like "I'm not sure how to act around you now that you've rejected me," and "Why won't you go out with me?" This will reek of desperation and will definitely make things super uncomfortable for both of you every time you come into contact with each other. If they do go out with you, it will be out of pity. But look on the bright side—at least they finally said yes!

101

★ **Suck it up and be mature.** This situation is only as awkward as you make it. If you act weird, nervous, and/or desperate, they'll act weird(er) in kind. If you act like you always have around them (and like nothing happened), they'll (be more likely to) follow your lead, and your interactions in the future will be unaffected. After all, your putting them on the spot by asking them out was awkward for them, too—they had to reject someone they see all the time. It will be a relief to them if you continue on normally, and they'll think better of you for it. Not being (outwardly) affected by a rejection from someone you see a lot is a sign of maturity and confidence in yourself and your value, and is very cool.

▶▶ **You're hanging out with your single, attractive fellow marathon-trainee and totally feel the romantic spark, so you move in for a smooch, only to find—when they push you away and look at you like you're crazy—that you completely misread the situation and that the sparks were one-sided. Yikes.**

More so than in most awkward situations, how you react here determines how awkward things get. Because this is an extremely embarrassing situation, it's easy to get bogged down in "oh my god that did *not* just happen" and fall down a shame spiral. Also, because you screwed up and misread the situation (which makes you look like an idiot) and got rejected on top of that, it's a double hit of embarrassment and shame for not realizing what was actually happening. Many of us, when faced with such intense levels of emotion, lash out—with anger, by trying to turn the situation around and blaming the person for leading us on, etc. These are douchebag moves and will only serve to turn a bad situation worse.

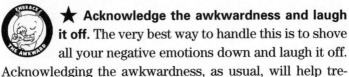 ★ **Acknowledge the awkwardness and laugh it off.** The very best way to handle this is to shove all your negative emotions down and laugh it off. Acknowledging the awkwardness, as usual, will help tremendously to relieve the tension.

Immediately follow this with an apology for misreading the situation, and promptly move on from this cesspit of awkward (i.e., don't dwell on what happened).

Something Awkward That (Might Have) Happened

>> AWKWARD MOMENTS WITH VOICEMAIL

Here's an example of a super-awkward first-date follow-up voicemail I received once. I'd gone out with "Rob" one time. It ended with lots of smiling and "let's definitely do this again's," and I had high hopes for future dates. I thought he was a cool guy . . . until I received these voicemails the morning after we went out.

4:14 AM: "Um, yeah . . . Hey, Sam. This is Rob. I just wanted to say that although I had a great time with you tonight, I just don't see this working out. I mean, I had a lot of fun, but I just don't think I can marry you. And if I can't marry you, there's no point in us continuing. Okay, well . . . 'Bye."

BTW, I had said *nothing* about marriage or even anything about actually committing to a second date. I have no idea where he was coming from on that.

4:17 AM: "Um, hi again. This is Rob . . . again. I just . . . I just can't believe you'd do that to me! How could you dump me after such a great date? I really liked you. You're such a bitch for doing this. How could you?!" [*Click.*]

. . . I hadn't talked to him.

103

4:21 AM: "Uh, yeah, hi. This is Rob. Again. Sorry about that—I just really like you, and I really want this to work. And I'm sorry about what I said about not marrying you. I could definitely marry you. In fact, let's do it. Do you want to go get married? [*Ten-second pause.*] Oh shit. I just asked you to marry me on your voicemail. That's weird, right? Call me back. Oh my GOD!" [*Click.*]

4:23 AM: "I could never marry a whore like you."

4:23:30 AM: "Sorry about that. I don't think you're a whore, or a bitch. I think you're great. K. Have a good night."

4:31 AM: "Seriously. Why aren't you calling me back? Who does that? You're an awful human being. I hope you die."

4:35 AM: "I don't really want you to die. How could I even have said that about my future wife? I think I love you. We're so perfect for each other. [*Sighs dramatically.*] But seriously, why aren't you calling me back?"

4:41 AM: "Yeah, hi—this is Rob, from the date tonight. I just wanted to say I had a really great time, and I'm really looking forward to seeing you again. But only if you call me back. Because otherwise, I'm going to come find you. . . . Just kidding. That was weird, wasn't it? Oh god, that was totally weird. Now you think I'm weird. Great. Perfect." [*Click.*]

Did he just forget the previous seven voicemails?

4:52 AM: "Seriously. Why don't you ever pick up your phone? Where are you? What are you doing?"

4:59 AM: "Okay, this really isn't going to work. I can't go out with some bitch who never returns my calls. Forget it."

And so it continued, for a grand total of seventeen voice mails, all received before 6:00 AM.

Needless to say, I didn't call him back. And since he worked at my favorite coffee shop, I suffered through a full two weeks of self-inflicted chai-latte deprivation before I gathered up the courage to face the awkward and go in there again.

Much to my relief, he acted like he'd never seen me before. I went with it.

When the crazy overtakes you, and you end up leaving a weird, awkwardly phrased, or totally insane voicemail.

Pretend it never happened. Call them a couple days later and pretend like everything is fine and you haven't left them any previous voicemails. If they bring it up, say that it must have been your roommate messing with them. You wouldn't ever do anything like that.

★ **Laugh it off.** Assuming you didn't completely lose it and leave a series of voicemails like my bat-shit-crazy-pants date, there's always the option of 'fessing up and laughing about it with them later. Something like the following will do wonders to (hopefully) put you back in your crush's good graces.

Let's say this is the voicemail you left: "Hey, Julie. I had a really good time tonight and just wanted to make sure I tie you down for our next date. Sound good? Call me."

Obviously, the phrasing can be interpreted to mean either that you'd like to see Julie for another date, or that you want to tie her up on your next date. Oops.

To recover, try a combination of humor, further awkwardness (it's endearing), and laughing at yourself. Something like this may work well either immediately thereafter, in a voicemail the next day, or in person, the next time you see her:

"Hey, Julie. So, I realized that my phrasing in the last voicemail I left you was, ah, well—it left a lot to the imagination, and I just want to say that what I meant was that I'd like to see you again . . . on another date. Your choice. And if you want me to tie you up, we can totally discuss that. Ha. Just kidding. Unless you liked that idea . . . [*Pause.*] K. Talk soon. Bye."

Also, remember that some voicemail systems have a press-1-to-accept menu that you'll hear once you finish talking. So, if you catch yourself leaving a crazy-town message, pray fervently that your crush has that feature, and perhaps the dating gods will listen.

▶▶ You're in bed with Jackie, and you just called her Melanie. In other words, you just screwed up while screwing.

This has the potential to be an epic cluster of awkward, and unfortunately, it happens on a fairly regular basis. Our brains are typically not running at full capacity in the heat of the moment, and sometimes we just screw up—especially when we're with a new partner after a longer-term situation, or when we've been doing a lot of fantasizing about someone else. . . .

Rarely, you'll get lucky, and the other person won't notice your slip-up because you mumbled or they weren't listening.

Sometimes they'll hear you (and you'll know they heard you), but they won't say anything because it's so awkward. Newer trysts are usually much more forgiving than long-term relationships, and brand-new partners in flings that haven't gotten serious may even find it entertaining.

And sometimes, you'll get confronted mid-coitus, and the situation will go from pleasant to a total disaster in a split second.

It's up to you whether you want to say anything (if you're not thrown into a confrontation). Respect dictates that you should say something, besides which, communication seems to be a healthier way to go than not—but if you're feeling like a jerk, technically you don't need to talk if they don't.

Dodge the Awkward Monster

In the future, to avoid such sexual disasters, use generic pronouns instead of their name if you need to address them mid-romp, or to let them know they're pleasing you. "You're so hot!" "Yeah, babe—that's it!" and "Sugar tits, you're the best!" all work equally as well as "Jackie, you're so hot!" "Yeah, John—that's it!" and "Susan, you're the best!"

If you are confronted, do not, under any circumstances, deny it. Apologize profusely. Show your partner you know their name by using it. State how much you like them and how much fun you have with them, and then make it up to them. Keep in mind they have a right to be pissed and that you might be blacklisted for a while.

After the dust has settled from the initial blowup, it may be worth taking some time to examine why you said someone else's name in the first place. Was it an honest mistake due to force of habit (as would be the case with a new fling after a long-term relationship—muscle memory and all that), or is your subconscious trying to tell you something?

Just a guess, but if you keep calling your boy-/girlfriend a name that's not theirs, it might be important to get to the root of why.

107

Awkward sex: It's on, but you can't get it up.

While all involved will understand that this occasionally happens (waaaay more often than anyone talks about, judging from the number of suggestions I received to include this one in this book), the relative frequency of it happening to other people doesn't usually help alleviate the awkwardness factor when it happens to you and it becomes apparent that things are going to have to be postponed until another time.

Drinking, drug use, and emotional upset (as well as a bevy of health problems) can all play a role in this. The first step to alleviating awkwardness as much as possible is to not freak out. Freaking out makes things way worse and is a total mood killer (whomever you're with may not know what to say or do to make you feel better, so your freaking out is not going to help). It's unlikely that your partner will not have noticed what's going on, so communicating to them about what's happening is way more mature than getting embarrassed and bailing.

The very best way to handle this is to let them know what the situation is via a simple, calm statement. Then apologize for having to change plans and suggest any number of other fun activities the two of you can do (that don't require the use of your member)—for example, giving each other full-body massages, making it a focus-on-your-partner night, telling each other your deepest, darkest fantasies for future playtime, cuddling while watching a scary movie, or getting your nerd on with a rousing game of Monopoly or Carcassonne.

You just suggested a secret sexual fantasy to your bedmate. They're horrified.

If it's a longer-term relationship, hopefully they'll recover quickly and come up with a more suitable supportive-significant-other reaction than the "Ew, gross!" or "Hell no!"

that sprang out of them when you mentioned your secret fantasy of girlfriend swapping with your best friend, Joe, and having an orgy next Tuesday night, or your secret desire to pee on them in the shower.

Things get awkward fast when we have a less-than-excited/supportive reaction to our deep dark secrets and desires. We're already feeling vulnerable, and a blatantly negative reaction to our innermost thoughts can result in extreme embarrassment, anxiety about what the other person thinks of us, and intense awkwardness.

If it's a longer relationship, it can feel like we've been deeply betrayed (and in a way, we have—revealing secrets in what we thought was a trusting, safe, and supportive environment only to have them rejected, or worse, is painful). As a result, our significant other will feel bad for making us feel bad, as well as feel conflicted about what to do with our revelation, while we feel any number of emotions: embarrassed, hurt, angry, and sad. The sum of all this confusion is an extremely awkward situation.

If it's a new relationship or a fling (or you simply don't care to get into it), a simple "Okay—I guess you're not into that!" with a laugh at your partner's strong reaction and a change of subject will do wonders for defusing the situation.

In longer relationships, although the instinct is to pull back and forget we ever said anything (kind of like with brain freeze—we just want it to go away), once it's out there, it's hard to ignore or forget about (on both sides), so not talking about it (or your feelings about their reaction) will likely produce some solid emotional festering. I'm going to go ahead and throw it out there that festering is unhealthy.

109

If, however, you can't let it go, talking is necessary. Try explaining (as calmly if possible) that although it's fine that your girl-/boyfriend doesn't want to participate in your far-fetched fantasy—you're not even sure Joe's girl-friend would be down, so it's unlikely it would ever happen anyway—their disgust for your thoughts hurts. It would have been far better if they'd just said they weren't interested. Once you feel heard and the two of you can move forward, discuss compromises—can the two of you explore some freakier porn together? Perhaps you'll find something you're both into.

 Awkward sex: Unequal libidos.

When your significant other wants it more than you do, it can turn something fun—sex—into something awkward. This blows. (No pun intended.)

Handling this, as with pretty much anything else in a relationship, requires communication. Libidos differ, so instead of having the times you both *do* want it turn into guilt-fests in which one partner berates the other for not wanting it enough, repeating "Wasn't that fun? We should do it more often," figure out a way to communicate and compromise.

Discussing your sex life (or lack thereof) can often be fraught with any number of emotions that may make things waaaaay awkward, including anxiety (over the health of the relationship), guilt (for wanting it too much or too little and not living up to your partner's expectations), and fear (of upsetting your partner by stating how you *really* feel).

To have a productive unequal-libido conversation, aim to make your find-a-solution talk as un-awkward as possible.

✻ Don't bring it up in bed, or anywhere else sexy. Bring it up some other time, when you're alone with your partner and you're comfortable—maybe while the two of you are walking the dog, maybe on a lazy Sunday afternoon when you're both hanging out at home.

* Make sure they know you love and respect them (by saying so).
* Say that you'd like to find a solution to something that's been on your mind recently.

Regardless of which side you're coming from (too much or too little), setting up a conversation in a safe, respectful, "let's find a solution" environment rather than a "things better change or else" environment will do wonders for reducing awkwardness and overly emotional reactions (remember the anxiety, guilt, and fear?). Then listen to your partner and try to understand why they want what they do.

Attempt a compromise—can you guys take sexy pictures for the hornier of the two to masturbate to when the other doesn't want to have sex? What about setting aside one day a week for an intimate night that doesn't involve sex, like a cuddling session or massage? That way, you're still physically close, but there's no pressure for sex. Putting everything out there so that sex, when it does happen, can be enjoyed without any pesky other emotions will make your relationship a whole lot less awkward. Yay!

You get caught heavily canoodling where you shouldn't even be playing, like on the office conference room table.

Depending on who caught you, you could be facing anything from heavy gossip to getting fired for inappropriate conduct. It's going to be pretty obvious to anyone walking in that you're having sex and not, despite what you've claimed, having your unzipped partner help you with your golf swing.

That said, depending on who caught you, you have some options:

111

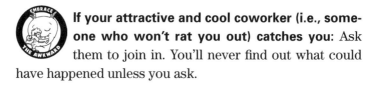 **If your attractive and cool coworker (i.e., some-
one who won't rat you out) catches you:** Ask
them to join in. You'll never find out what could
have happened unless you ask.

**If your boss, who hates you and is looking for
any excuse to fire you, catches you:** Continue.
Finish loudly and dramatically while giving your
boss the finger. If you're going to burn the bridge, you might
as well use a giant, propane-powered flamethrower.

**If it's your shy and reserved coworker, who after
catching you, looks like they just swallowed a
spider:** Stop, cover yourself up, and apologize to
them.

**If the guy from the company that shares your
building catches you:** Give him a thumbs-up and
a grin as you continue, and then motion for him to
shut the door on his way out.

▶▶ **You just caught your boss getting frisky on her
desk.**

As this definitely qualifies as inappropriate behavior on the
part of your boss, by stumbling across her off-hours antics,
you've now come into possession of knowledge she's probably going to want to keep quiet.

**Find her later and assure her you won't say any-
thing.** If she can trust you to keep this secret,
maybe she'll trust you more in general. Also, she'll
owe you one so maybe the next time you call in sick when
everyone knows you're hungover, she'll let it slide.

Blackmail her for a raise. Although potentially effective, this will do nothing for her opinion of you and will put you on her shit list. Definitely an at-your-own-risk move, this is a surefire way to secure life-long bad juju for yourself.

 Tell all your coworkers what you saw. Expect to occupy a permanent position on her shit list.

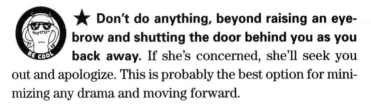 ★ **Don't do anything, beyond raising an eyebrow and shutting the door behind you as you back away.** If she's concerned, she'll seek you out and apologize. This is probably the best option for minimizing any drama and moving forward.

You just got caught masturbating.

Whether it's a family member, roommate, friend, coworker (really?), or a random who catches you, it's going to be awkward. Yeah, everyone does it, but that doesn't really make it any less universally OMFG or WTF if you get caught with your hands in your pants (or your pants off, as the case may be).

In all situations, unless you're caught by your significant other and they're used to and accepting of joining in your special time, you should not:

1. Keep masturbating, no matter how close you are to the fireworks
2. Ask whoever caught you to lend a hand
3. Make a mess and then not clean it up.

If you were somewhere reasonable when you got caught—like the privacy of your own bedroom or bathroom—you do have a right to be mad about the interruption. (Doesn't anyone *knock* anymore?)

Dodge the Awkward Monster

Next time, lock the door.

<<

If, however, you were anywhere public—your office, a communal space in your house, or someplace where it's not unlikely someone would find you (your car, for example?)—you have no right to be mad and should, the next time you feel the urge, get yourself behind a locked door.

In all cases, you should immediately stop, cover yourself up, apologize to whoever found you, and if you were somewhere totally inappropriate, look ashamed and be prepared to end up on a sex offender list.

▶▶ **You just caught your mom or dad masturbating.**

However disturbing this may be, try to remember that Mom and Dad are human and, like all humans, have sexual urges. The best way to handle this one is to turn on your heel and walk the other way. Don't bring it up with them. Don't allow them to have yet another sex talk with you. Just move on.

▶▶ **You just walked in on your boss masturbating in his/her office.**

Lend them a left hand. After all, you're already their right hand. . . . Actually, don't.

Treat this like walking in on your parents. Don't say anything, don't stick around, don't mention it again—just turn around and leave them to it, shutting the door behind you.

There's absolutely no reason you need to bring it up, ever, but if they bring it up to apologize or offer some lame excuse for what they were "actually" doing, accept the apology and the excuse (even if you both know that you know exactly what they were doing) and file the experience away in your "I hope I never see that again" file.

You just got caught staring at the boobs, butt, abs, or other sexually pleasing features of someone you're not dating (like your boss).

In most cases, even if all parties involved are aware that you were fantasizing about them, it's far more awkward to acknowledge the situation.

In most cases, once the person has gotten your attention by means of a cleared throat in combination with a raised eyebrow and a glare, all that's required to acknowledge the situation and convey your silent apology is your sheepish grin—along with your obvious heavy blushing, floor staring, and/or foot shuffling.

For example, if instead you do the following, the situation becomes tangible, and you can bet that you're shortly going to be headed to HR for a talk and/or that things will be weird between you and your boss from this point forward.

Your boss: "Do you have that report ready?"

You, *staring at your female boss's chest, somewhat visible in her V-neck sweater*: "..."

Your boss: "Jeff?"

You, *finally noticing someone is saying your name*: "Huh? What?"

Your boss: "The report, Jeff. Are you okay? You seem distracted."

You: "Um, yeah. I have the report. And I apologize. This is really awkward, but I was staring at your chest—that's why I was distracted."

Your boss: "..."

You, *staring at the wall just over her right shoulder so you don't have to look her in the eye or have your gaze's trajectory be mistaken for anywhere else*: "..."

Awkward silence ensues.

Dodge the Awkward Monster

In the future, don't stare at your boss's boobs.

▶▶ **Your father walks in on you and your significant other having sex.**

After you're done freaking out and watching your parental unit do the fastest backpedal you've ever seen, take a minute to reflect on the fact that this encounter was probably much more disturbing and awkward for him than for you.

To remedy the awkward pauses that now haunt any interactions you and your father have, reference the encounter as obliquely as possible ("You know that thing you saw the other day?") and follow it immediately with an apology ("I'm sorry about that"). Then continue about your business. If he wants to talk about it (like to make sure you know about condoms), he'll bring it up again. If he doesn't, he won't. Done and done.

In the future, lock the door if you're planning on heading to Frisky-town while under your parents' roof.

Drama with Roommates

Nothing gets under people's skin faster than roommate issues. After all, home is where we go to decompress, to recharge, and to get away from the craziness of our lives. And because in the major cities of the world it's ridiculously expensive to live by ourselves, roommates are a fact of life for many of us. Add to this the difficulty of finding someone whose cleaning/living/eating habits match yours, the fact that we all have our own way of doing things, and the basic truth that at heart we all think our way is the best way, and finding viable living partners becomes very challenging.

Although many of us have the best intentions to communicate and not act like fourth-graders on the playground when dealing with roommates, in reality we fall far short.

Passive-aggressiveness seems to be the non-communication plan of choice for roommates, across the board. Because many of us battle at work, with our significant others, and with family on a regular basis, it's much easier to let things slide and just build up a giant pile of steaming resentment at home.

Plus, communication takes work and patience, and unless all roommates are on board with actively communicating and cooperating, it's often pretty awkward to call someone out on their behavior at home.

All that said, it's a far better deal to just communicate, however awkward it may seem. Being easygoing and picking your battles is a major asset in opening the roommate pool to a size that allows you to actually find someone you're compatible with. Be extremely communicative about what you want and what's important to you, and realize that cooperation, compromise, and respect are all vital if you want to keep the peace at home. Duh, right?

Roommate hell avoided.

You just walked in on your roommate handcuffed to her bed, being ravished like in a romance novel . . . in your shared room.

Let's say you come home early from work or class or whatever, and are looking forward to an afternoon nap. You've lived in your apartment long enough to not need to look where you're going to get to your room, and so you're focused on browsing the new Victoria's Secret catalogue as you walk from the front door to your back bedroom.

Upon arriving, you note that the door to your bedroom is shut, but you don't think much of it and walk in, at which point you hear a squeak of surprise from the opposite corner of the room, where your roommate's bed is located. Looking up, you find her handcuffed to her bed and see the naked ass of a guy pointed in your direction as he does things to her that she was obviously enjoying before you so rudely interrupted. She's now staring at you with a look that can be mistaken for nothing other than "Get the fuck out," but you're so surprised by what you've walked in on that you remain rooted to the spot.

Eventually, not knowing what else to do, you backpedal out the door you just came through, shut it, and spend the next hour unsuccessfully trying to erase the image of her boyfriend's naked ass that's been seared into your brain.

What do you do?

★ **Pretend like nothing happened.** You could, once you recover from the shock of having intimate knowledge of the scattering of moles on both your roommate and her man of the hour, act like nothing happened. However, once you've seen it, you can't ever go back. There's not a shot in hell you won't keep seeing them naked whenever you look at them from now on.

Get even. You could try to one-up her and invite your favorite plaything over for an afternoon romp when you know your roommate is likely to walk in. Mature? No. Effective, in a passive-aggressive fashion? Yes.

Dodge the Awkward Monster

If you're sharing a room with someone and you both like to romp with your respective partners, the key

is prevention. Some sort of communication and compromise on what can happen, where, and when and a signal system to prevent unwanted interruptions is entirely necessary. Although it may be overkill to really talk through every possible situation, at least discussing the common ones will prevent some potential epic awkwardness that could arise from walking in on your roommate getting it from behind or accidentally witnessing her spanking skills.

In the future, use the sock signal. In age-old tradition, a scarf or sock on the door is a great signal for "there's something happening right now," but this can get really annoying if they forget to remove it after they're done.

Come up with a schedule. Discussing the possibility of a pre-set schedule, and/or allowing the other roommate to enter the room briefly to grab what they need (when the room is otherwise in use), will do wonders for keeping the peace. Also, a heads-up if the plan is to have a "friend" over that night and/or an ability to compromise on where the romping happens (is the couch available?) helps.

★ **Laugh it off.** If all the preplanning fails, and you do end up walking in on your roommate and/or their b-/gf in a compromising position, realize that it happens and that presumably you've all seen the equipment on display before. Get what you need from the room and avert your eyes. Bonus points awarded for saying something like "Enjoy that" or "Nice ass" as you leave.

You can't sleep because your housemate has crazy, screaming sex every night.

Many apartments inhabited by the twenty- to thirty-something crowd with roommates are not the insulated, soundproof, loft-ceilinged six-bedroom/five-bath mansions we'd like them to be. Instead, their construction is more often than not the same age as the glint in your father's eye when he saw your mother for the first time. As for sound-proofing? Well, there isn't any.

Listening to your housemate get some, whether or not you're currently getting any, is entertaining (at least for a while) at best and really annoying at worst. On a repeat basis, it has the potential to get really old, really fast.

Fight fire with fire. Find yourself a vocal partner of your own, or if that doesn't seem feasible, buy some raunchy porn and turn all the speakers in your room toward their bedroom to maximize the noise directed at them. Then as soon as your housemate starts getting busy, get busier. And louder. Your neighbors won't complain, I swear.

★ **Make other noise.** Every time you hear the porn sound track start up down the hallway, turn up your music to epic levels to drown out the moans, put on some noise-canceling headphones and Zen out, or start humming and putting your fingers in your ears.

Be annoying. Park yourself in the hallway outside their bedroom and bang on their door every time you hear a moan, or sing Christmas carols, hymns, or Disney songs at the top of your lungs to put them out of the mood.

★ **Talk about it.** Have a grown-up chat with your roommate about the noise level of their sexual escapades and request that they either keep it down or put on some moan-drowning music of their own.

When your neighbor, with whom you share a bedroom wall, appears to be in training for the porn Olympics.

This situation is more complicated than a similar situation with a roommate because you don't have as much clout (presumably you're not going halfsies on the rent of your neighbor's apartment). The options are much the same as with a roommate, except expect less cooperation if you try and have a mature chat with them.

If it keeps happening, you have the added option of a) complaining to your landlord or b) calling the cops and reporting a noise complaint.

 ★ Or you could make lemonade out of lemons and invite some friends over to play a drinking game with every slap, moan, and thump you hear.

Something Awkward That (Might Have) Happened

>> UNFORTUNATELY TIMED PARENTS

My friend Beth was home for Thanksgiving during college. Her dad had headed out for the afternoon to run some errands, so Beth called up an old "friend" from high school, Jeff, to hang out for the afternoon. They decided to take advantage of the empty house and enjoy some reminiscing of a physical nature on the couch in her dad's living room. Things were just getting interesting (he wasn't wearing pants, she was topless) when they heard the front door open. Since the living room was in full view of the front door, they had about two seconds to grab the only thing within reach, a heavy wool afghan knitted by Beth's

121

great-grandmother, and throw it over themselves, covering both of them up to the neck.

A few seconds later, Beth's dad walked in and plopped down on the couch next to them.

Beth's dad: "Hi, guys."

Beth, *trying to look like she isn't topless under the blanket*: "Hi, Dad. You're home early."

Jeff, *trying not to squirm*: "Hi there, Mr. Brewer."

Beth's dad, who Beth swears would have put her in a convent if he'd ever caught her doing anything more than kissing under his roof, noted that they were both covered with a heavy blanket when it was seventy degrees outside (she lived in Southern California): "Yeah—they didn't have what I needed. . . . Beth, are you okay? It's beautiful out. Why are you huddled up inside under a blanket?"

Beth: "Um, yeah—I wasn't feeling well. Jeff came over to keep me company for the afternoon."

Beth's dad: "That's too bad. You mind if I join in? I wouldn't mind watching a movie. That's what you guys were going to do, right?"

Beth and Jeff, *in unison*: "Yep. That's what we were doing."

Beth's dad, *not noticing the too-eager response and squinting at the row of DVDs on the shelf above the TV*: "Good then, it's settled. How about the last *Lord of the Rings*? I haven't seen it in a long time."

Beth, *gulping*: "Uh, yeah. That sounds great."

Beth's dad: "Jeff? You okay with *Lord of the Rings*?"

Jeff: "Um, yep. That sounds great."

Beth's dad: "Okay, then. *Return of the King* it is."

He got up to put the movie in and noticed Beth's bra and shirt and Jeff's jeans on the floor near the couch. Noticing him noticing their clothes, they both started sweating. After a pause, Beth's dad continued:

"Beth, if you've got company over, you should really try to clean up a little better. I'll just put your clothes in the laundry room for you—how's that? Do you guys want anything? Water?"

Beth, *going pale*: "Uh . . . um . . . you can leave the clothes, Dad. Sorry. I'll pick them up later."

Beth's dad: "Oh, it's no trouble. I'll drop them off on my way to the kitchen. Water?"

Beth, *not believing that this is really happening*: "Um, yeah, that'd be great."

Beth's dad picked up her bra and shirt and Jeff's jeans and headed out of the room. Beth and Jeff could only stare at each other in horror at what the next three hours would hold. And hold they did—since they had no way of going to the bathroom, they had to sit there and pretend everything was fine as they sat mostly naked, three feet away from Beth's dad, the sworn enforcer of convent-dom.

Beth relayed to me later that her dad, concerned that she was cold, turned up the heat halfway through the movie so that, besides the already extreme awkwardness of the situation (and the nervous sweat that was causing), she and Jeff were both sweating like crazy from being overheated under the super-heavy blanket. Apparently by the time her dad eventually left them on the couch after the movie ended, the couch under them was drenched. After her dad exited the room, three hours and twenty-nine minutes after walking in, Beth was able to sprint to the laundry room and safely grab their clothes, and their little tryst remained undiscovered.

She swears, however, that to this day (a few years after the fact), she won't even kiss her husband on that couch, it holds such traumatic memories.

When laughing forcefully near your crush ends badly . . .

(page 137)

When Champagne/ Tequila/Beer Takes Over

When fun pushes responsibility out of the way and we think it's a super-good idea to combine three bottles of wine, a cell phone, a camera, and some pent-up emotion, it's like ringing the dinner bell for the Awkward Monster.

So, the next time it seems like a solid plan to drunk-text our ex, tell our crazy coworker what we really think of them, or partake in an ill-advised hookup at the office holiday party, the following chapter will equip us to handle the fallout.

It's Monday and time for work. However, Saturday night's debauchery—in the form of "PENIS" written in permanent marker across your forehead—is still very visible, despite much time devoted to removing it.

 ★ **Lie and play the sympathy card.** Cover your forehead with bandages, and tell everyone you fell and cut your head over the weekend.

Just lie. Get another permanent marker and draw a rectangle around the "PENIS." Now fill it in. When people ask, tell them it's a new dermatological treatment for some precancerous patches and you're just doing your preventative due diligence.

Try to get away with it. Leave the "PENIS" and put on a beanie, pulling it down far enough to cover up the letters. When your boss asks you to take off the hat, apologize ahead of time and say you were mugged this weekend, but instead of beating you up, the thief took your wallet and wrote on your face.

★ **Be cool.** Wear a hat and when asked why you're wearing one, explain that your friends played a prank on you this weekend, and for the sake of keeping the office PC, you'd appreciate it if your boss wouldn't mind your wearing this hat for the next five to seven days, until the prank wears off.

Dodge the Awkward Monster

Next time, don't pass out with your shoes on when you've had one too many at the party. Everyone knows shoes on equals open season for markers on exposed skin.

A friend drank too much the other night and blacked out, during which time he confessed while crying that he cheated on his girlfriend two years ago, but that it happened when he was drunk, it was a onetime thing, it was a huge mistake, and it won't ever, ever happen again because he loves her. She's a good friend of yours. He clearly doesn't remember saying anything to you, and now you're stuck in the middle of a really shitty secret.

Forget you ever heard anything. You were drinking, too, so it's possible you're not remembering what he said correctly. . . . Now if you could just convince yourself of that.

★ **Tell him that you know.** This is their business and not your secret to tell, especially since he swore in liquid-truth mode that he wouldn't ever do it again. Leaving her in ignorant, blissful, untarnished love with him and leaving him to bear the guilt and pain of betraying her is quite possibly a better deal for her than him telling her about something that happened a long time ago and that won't ever happen again.

So, let him know you know, and to keep him honest, tell him that if it ever happens again, you're telling her.

Something Awkward
That (Might Have) Happened

>> DRINKING + BLIND DATING = BAD

This story is going to make you think I'm an obnoxious lush, but it's awkward, so I want to include it here as a cautionary tale. In my defense, I was in college—where everyone makes many ill-advised decisions under the influence of copious amounts of alcohol, right?

A party for which I needed a date had come up, so a friend set me up with her date's friend so we could all go to the party together. As it turns out, my date couldn't make the pre-party and had to meet us at the actual party, so he missed the heavy drinking (that seemed like a superfantastic idea at the time) that my friend, her date, and I did before we left for the party.

I'm a lightweight in the drinking department, so my memory of the evening stopped well before we ever left my friend's apartment to go to the party. As a result, although I met my date and apparently had a great time dancing with him, talking to him, and hanging out, I remembered nothing of the evening—not what he looked like and not what we talked about. His impression of me (delivered through my friend's date) was that I was fun and "just a little tipsy"—apparently he had no idea how much I'd had to drink. Embarrassed by my behavior, I didn't try to get in touch with him after the party.

I went to another party (sober this time) a couple weeks later and saw this cute guy by the grill. Seeing as we were the only two people on the patio, I started talking to him. He was acting really strange and off-putting, so eventually, after several failed conversation attempts with the standard questions of "So, do you go here, too?" and "What's your major?" I said something like "Well, I guess I'll head back inside. It doesn't seem like you want company."

His response? "That's because you pretending you don't know me is really weird."

My response: ". . . ?"

I was completely mystified as to what he was talking about. I'd never seen him before, and I would have remembered him if I had—he was really cute. I said as much, at which point he told me he was my date to *that* party, and it all clicked into place.

He wasn't at all pleased that a) I'd thought it had been a good idea to get blacked-out drunk before I even met him on our first date, or that b) I didn't remember him or any of the apparently many deep conversations we had. Needless to say, he didn't want to hang out with me again. Date fail.

Embarrassing? Definitely. Awkward? You bet. Especially since he started dating one of my other close friends shortly after my grill-side enlightenment and I started seeing him around more frequently.

I found out over the course of the next several weeks (when I would try to be polite and talk to him when we were all out together) that everything I seemed to ask him, he'd already told me. His response to me ("Yeah—I already told you that") every time this happened eventually turned into a rather-embarrassing-for-me but amusing-for-everyone-else inside joke in our friend circle: Every time any of us encountered a question we didn't have an answer to (ranging from what someone wanted for dinner to what the time was), we'd merely have to say, "Yeah—I already told you that," providing hours of endless giggling at my expense.

Your date for the office holiday party gets wasted and tells your boss every bad thing you've ever said about him/her.

The golden combination of alcohol-induced lowered inhibitions and non-functioning social filters is a fantastic awkwardness generator . . . especially at work functions.

Your first order of business is to apologize for your date's behavior and get her away from your boss so she can't do any more damage.

★ **Apologize. Deny.** Then apologize again and blame your date's word-vomit on her one-night stand with the wine. Pretend, with every acting bone you've got in your body, that you have no idea what she's talking about and that your best guess is she must be confusing you with her roommate, who hates his boss and on a very frequent basis says many of the things your date repeated tonight.

Apologize a third time for her behavior (since you recognize that, as her date, you're responsible for her), and finish with a heartfelt compliment about your boss's appearance. Make this sound like a deliberate attempt at kissing ass (for example, "Have I told you how dapper you look tonight, sir?" or, "You look great tonight, by the way"). This will be a funny icebreaker and awkward-diffuser since it will be taken exactly how you meant it, as a brown-nosing, "please forgive my blunder" compliment.

With any luck, your boss will chuckle and tell you to reevaluate your choice of date in the future, and then go about his/her night.

▶▶ **You drank just enough at the office holiday party to make it seem like a good idea to spill to a gossipy coworker your too-honest and very snarky assessments of everyone in the office.**

This is one of those wait-and-see situations, where you'll have to handle the fallout as it hits you. Some people will confront you; most won't. This latter group may either passive-aggressively let you know that their feelings are hurt (for example, by ignoring you or deliberately skipping you for the office lunch order), or file away your bitchy observations and fester about it but never mention anything to you.

If, however, you're confronted about your snark:

★ **Blame your coworker.** Take the stance that the gossipy coworker was the drunk one and you never said what she said you said. Assure the person with the hurt feelings that you're sorry they heard a vicious rumor but that it's simply not true.

Confess, apologize, and repeat your (slightly reworded) snark to their face. Treat this as an opportunity to work through any problems you may have with people. Apologize for the way that they found out (secondhand sucks), but say that, yeah, you called them an asshole because it really bothers you that they took credit for the idea you had to disallow bit-torrent-sharing sites in the office to solve the recurring problem of people downloading viruses onto the work servers. Expect varying degrees of success in your problem-solving crusade.

★ **Apologize.** Admit that, yes, you were drunk, so whatever they heard was just the alcohol talking, and no, you don't really think that the nineties called and want your coworker's hair back. Tell the hurt feelings that you've had a really rough year and that you were taking it out on everyone else at the party. Apologize again, and promise that you've enrolled in some new yoga classes and that you have high hopes you'll be feeling more Zen (and less bitchy) very soon.

151

▶▶ You got drunk last night and made out with your friend's crush.

 Stay quiet. She's going to be hurt when she finds out, so in the interest of avoiding hurting her (at least right away), you can wait and cross your fingers that she never finds out about your drunken betrayal of the friend code. If she ends up with this guy, what happened will surface eventually, but maybe by that point she won't care because he's with her anyway. If you can save her experiencing pain now, you will—even if it means potentially jeopardizing your friendship with her later on (when she finds out you've been lying by omission for the last five years).

★ **Tell her.** If, however, you can't handle the crushing weight of your guilt, you can sit her down, buy her some coffee, and confess, and then immediately grovel, apologize, beg for her forgiveness, and assure her that you know how badly you screwed up and it will never happen again.

Your continued friendship is more important than some random make-out session, so although she won't like hearing it and the conversation will probably suck, being honest and remorseful is a better bet than hiding it and having it come to light later. An up-front and honest apology can do wonders for keeping things in a good place with all relationships.

If he decides to pursue you instead of her after the drunken make-out session: Be prepared to lose your friend for a bit while she gets over finding out a) her crush likes her best friend instead of her and b) said best friend made out with him.

Drunk texting (drexting)

Nothing ruins a day (or night, or next day) faster than sending a drunk text (and then regretting it when you're sober enough to realize what you've done). Liquid truth in the form of digital, permanent "ink" in 160 characters or less: Ouch . . . and it always seems like such a good idea at the time.

There are three categories of drunk texting, all of them probably ill-advised (there is the argument that in some cases, the door of communication could be pushed open by said texts, but I digress):

1. **Angry, vindictive, mean, bridge-burning texts.** For example, to your ex:
   * "I lied when I said your penis was huge."
   * "I cheated on you."
   * "I always thought your best friend was hotter than you."
   * "FYI, my new boy-/girlfriend is way better in bed than you ever were."

2. **Confession texts.** For example:
   * To your ex: "I'm still in love with you."
   * To your current crush, whom you've hung out with once in a large group: "I love you."
   * To your boss: "I love looking at your ass during staff meetings."

3. **Texts that were supposed to go to someone else** but in your merlot-/Corona-/Cuervo-addled brain, you failed to notice the "to" before you hit "send."
   * "I can't believe Cindy doesn't realize she's being cheated on—what an idiot," supposed to go to your best friend, Dan, but sent to Cindy.

133

✳ "Anna is so hot. Like the fist of an angry god, I'd hit that,"✳ supposed to go to your friend Brian, but went to your girlfriend instead. Oops.

Although it is *possible* that your text didn't go through or never made it to its intended destination—after all, SMS is not 100 percent reliable, and sometimes our texts disappear without a trace, like socks in a dryer—in reality, the texts that we would give our left eye to undo are the ones that always go through, right?

Depending on the type of truth told, you certainly have the option of staying silent and seeing if the receiver says anything (as may be the case when you send an ill-advised confession of love). Or you could bring it up the next time you see them.

With love confessions, for example, bringing your message up to the object of your Cuervo-addled affection has an equal chance of being:

a. Funny ("Haha—isn't it funny that I told you I loved you?")
b. Totally awkward (especially if it's someone who doesn't feel the same way and you've just forced them into the "I don't like you that way" conversation)
c. Fantastic ("OMG, I love you, too!")

Gamble away.

And of course, there's always the "my friend stole my phone" excuse, which although lame, may work in some circumstances, like with your un-tech-savvy (but callipygian) boss.

134

....
✳ Thanks for the quote, Dan. ☺

In cases of Freudian-slip trash-talking texts, the stand-up option is to call or meet up with the unintended receiver, apologize for any ramifications of your night of debauchery (or finger slip), and repair the damage as best you can. Be prepared to lose a friend. It's pretty shitty to find out that someone you thought was your friend is texting people about the things they don't like about you, no matter how merited the complaints might be.

On rare occasions, these texting slipups have been known to start a conversation that can clear the air and renew a relationship, but be prepared to deal with some seriously hurt feelings before that can happen.

And when you meant to send the text to Brian about how hot Anna is but you accidentally sent it to your girlfriend, don't be a douche—apologize to her and handle the fallout as best you can, remembering that although you may have just been joking around with Brian, it's going to look like a way bigger deal to your girlfriend because it's *in writing*. Provide your girlfriend with lots of "I'm sorry"s, lots of attention to assure her that you're not going to run off with Anna (assuming that's the case), and lots of patience as you let her work through her anger with you for being such a jackass. Good luck.

Food and beer spraying: When eating, drinking, and laughing join forces.

Spraying beer (or water or Coke or any other liquid you might be drinking) in the company of those who aren't going to forgive you as quickly as your friends might is an unfortunate situation, and it happens to the best of us. When we get nervous (like when we're on a date or trying to impress the boss), we tend to put more force into laughter than we normally do, and if we happen to be drinking something at the time? Behold the instant beer fountain.

135

I've been on the receiving end of a beer spray more than once, and although it's not an ideal situation, it hasn't ever not been funny—I've always been among friends when it happens. That said, I can imagine very clearly some situations where it would fall far more in the awkward bucket than the funny bucket: spraying your boss, your grandmother, the hot girl/guy you just met, the bride. . . . If you spray someone who will most definitely not find it amusing (like the bride and her $15,000 dress at her wedding), unlike with your friends, humor probably isn't the best way to go about alleviating the awkwardness. Your best (and only) option is to grab some napkins, help her get to the bathroom to clean up, and apologize as many times as it takes for her to know that you're truly, truly sorry for soaking her with mouth beer.

The thing about a sudden drenching (especially when the liquid has been in someone's mouth first) is that it kills any effort previously made to look good: hair, makeup, clothes. It's also pretty off-putting for the more germaphobic. Some brides will be more forgiving than others, so you can expect anything from a laugh (after she's done cleaning up) to a full-on breakdown (weddings are stressful and can very easily produce disproportionate reactions).

If you spray the hot girl on your first date together, repeat as you would with the bride, but with the option of laughing with her once you grab some napkins and apologize. As bad as this seems on a first date, it makes it memorable and so far into bad-date territory that it may actually serve as a bonding experience and give you both an icebreaker and a reason to laugh together (assuming she's not too high-maintenance). And if she sprays you, it's because you were super funny. Win.

However, if you're in a situation where it's just so incredibly awkward it's too much to handle, sometimes the only option besides crying and running away is to laugh (like when you spray your boss at the office holiday party)—although you may want to wait and see if they crack a smile first. Acknowledging the humor (and the awkwardness) in the situation after you've expressed a sincere apology may be a welcome show of confidence that your boss will dig (more so than you crying in embarrassment or quitting on the spot because you can't look them in the face again). Then again, you may end up on your boss's shit list and on thin ice for the foreseeable future.

Something Awkward That (Might Have) Happened

>> CRUSH FAIL

Although it's not alcohol related, the following fits here nicely, given the above discussion of sprayage of things previously in one's mouth.

I had a crush on this boy in high school, and one completely awesome Tuesday (at least until it wasn't), he deigned to talk to me during morning break. The first two minutes were spent making somewhat awkward small talk over the bagels we were both eating. I loved every second.

I was nervous because I liked him and so was laughing more and harder than usual. As a result, when he said something mildly funny, instead of chuckling like a normal person, I ended up exhaling in laughter so exuberant that the chunk of bagel and cream cheese I'd been chewing flew out of my mouth, smacking into his face right below his left eye. Gross, yes. Embarrassing, definitely. Awkward? Words don't begin to describe.

I think he said something like "Ew! Gross!" wiped his face with his sleeve, and bailed. Yay me. Crush fail.

When a compliment turns into an accidental in-your-face insult . . .

(page 168)

Miscommunication and "Oh Shit!" Moments

There are times in life when "Oh shit!" is the only thing we can say, such as situations where we get caught doing something we're not supposed to be doing (or when we assume that our boss will think it's funny we retorted with "That's what your mom said" to their request to "Please make sure you find a stiff cover. I don't want the document to feel floppy"). "Oh, shit!" is also an appropriate response when we'd rather voluntarily repeat middle school than spend one more second in a certain situation, such as being stuck in a ski-resort gondola with our ex and their new (extremely attractive) significant other. All these occasions suck. All are awkward.

And all are covered here so that the next time we experience them, we're better equipped to handle our self-made hell.

 You just spilled your entire glass of pinot on your girlfriend's parents' new white suede couch at your first Thanksgiving with her family.

Step 1: Apologize. Apologize again. Be sincere.

Step 2: Since someone will have run to get towels, take charge of the situation while that's happening and look up "how to remove red wine from a white suede couch" on your phone. Contemplate, while the answer is loading, whether or not you should be concerned that your girlfriend's parents just bought a white suede couch (who does that?) and move on. Then while you're helping with the mopping up, tell them you just looked up the best way to remove red wine from suede and that with warm water, dish soap, and quick action, you should be able to successfully and completely remove the stain.

Step 3: Acknowledge the awkwardness of the situation: Namely, you're trying your best to impress them because you love their daughter, and here you are, causing problems already. Hopefully her parents will laugh.

Step 4: Once the stain is gone, shake her father's hand and tell him you promise never to sit on his couch with red wine again.

Remain confident and calm and don't freak out. Once the problem is fixed, you should be in the clear. After all, it was your quick actions on the interwebs that led everyone to the correct path for getting the couch back to its blindingly white glory.

140

If, by chance, the stain did not come out, offer to pay for the couch to be cleaned (but only do so if you can actually pay for it!). Her parents will probably say no, but they'll appreciate the offer.

Dealing with forced proximity to someone you'd hoped to never see again: You're stuck in traffic and realize the person that's been in the car next to you for the last fifteen minutes (and staring at you) is the person with whom you went on a blind date two weeks ago and never called back.

Silently curse the dating gods for placing you in this position, and then do one of the following:

Ignore them. Be super focused on programming your radio, singing along with your radio once you've located a good song, or counting the change in your coin catcher.

Stare back, deadpan. Not many people can handle a direct stare-down, and most will back down pretty quickly if you keep it up. Don't smile, don't frown—just stare at them. This will freak them out, unless they're better at it than you and you lose. Then it will just be awkward.

Wave and smile. Act like you don't know why they're mouthing "Fuck you!" Roll down your window and ask how they are. If they accept a conversation and ask why you didn't call them back, pretend you didn't know you were supposed to—that you thought *they* were supposed to call *you*. Be prepared to prolong future awkwardness by ignoring their calls again.

★ **Acknowledge their presence with a half-wave and wry smile.** These gestures let them know you realize that it's awkward. This is honest and straightforward and the most respectful way to deal with the fact you're being faced with someone you didn't treat very well.

▶▶ **You run into the person you just dumped, in the produce section of the grocery store. It's only been an hour since you left them crying in the coffee shop.**

 ★ **Acknowledge, then avoid.** Honestly, the most humane thing to do is that half-wave, half-smile thing that says, "I realize this is awkward, and again—I'm sorry for hurting you," and then leave them alone, even going so far as to head to another part of the store and purposely avoid them for the rest of the time you're there.

After all, if you did say hi, what would you follow up with?

A thoughtlessly honest question: "How are you feeling since I dumped you?" (Awkward . . .)

A pompously honest question: "Is your day getting any better?" (Even more awkward, since it could be taken as you being a pompous jerk, even if you were honestly just inquiring as to how their day has been.)

★ **A deflection:** "You should check out the kumquats—they're in season." (Random enough that it may jolt them out of the shock of seeing you again so soon, so this could be an option. . . .)

If they initiate conversation, go with it for as long as it's pleasant. If they're angry or spitting venom at you, it's better to repeat your apology for hurting them and bail. Constructive conversation and healing rarely happen immediately after dropping a bomb like "I think we should break up," so save them (and you) the humiliation of getting upset in the

142

middle of the apples or the potential hurt of hurling insults you don't really mean, and postpone the rehashing of what went wrong for a time of smoother, calmer waters, when everyone's emotions are a little less whitecapped.

You've been leaving voicemails for someone every few days for the last month, and all your calls have gone unreturned. You just ran into them at the coffee shop.

 ★ **Don't mention the ignored voicemails.** They'll wonder why you aren't bringing up their bad behavior, and if you maintain a happy, upbeat attitude and tell a funny story about something that happened recently (to fill what could be a totally awkward silence), it will seem like you're so busy, you didn't even *notice* that they didn't return your calls.

Best case, they'll feel guilty and bring up the non-returned voicemails themselves, with an excuse as to why they've been ignoring you. At that point, you can either play it cool and act like it's no big deal they haven't called you back, or further the lie that you've been so busy you didn't even notice by saying something like "I didn't even notice you didn't call!", then dive in and bring up whatever you've been wanting to talk to them about.

★ **Acknowledge the awkwardness.** In an awkward situation like this where you both know what's going on (they've ignored you and you know it), acknowledging the awkwardness with a "So . . . this is awkward," followed by a friendly "I'm not going to go crazy on you for not returning my calls" smile, will probably be enough in most cases to defuse the awkwardness. When you, as the slighted person, avoid making things even more

143

awkward with a direct confrontation and, as a bonus, give you both a reason to laugh, it will be much appreciated and will allow the two of you to more easily talk openly, which presumably is what you're ultimately after.

Put on your crazy eyes and say "I've fooooouuuuuunnnd you!" in a high-pitched voice, while running toward the person. Because this is both creepy and awkward, follow it up with a laugh, a light punch on the shoulder, and an "OMG, I'm totally joking!" You'll look crazy, but it gets right to the point and may frazzle them enough they'll either just be honest about why they've been ignoring you (like they think you're crazy . . .) or provide you with some BS excuse ("What do you mean? Have you been looking for me? I haven't heard from you in a month . . .") to explain their silence.

Then again, this (extremely) escalated awkwardness may make them laugh, break through the awkwardness that you're both feeling, and open the door for a real conversation that could have a non-awkward positive outcome (they thought you were crazy, but now they can see you were only joking . . .).

▶▶ **You run into your recent ex while out and about, and they're with someone new.**

This is never easy, regardless of who did the dumping. And if it's the first or second time you've seen them since the breakup, there's bound to be a volcano of emotion you'll need to deal with. This makes it very challenging to act normally and like you're totally over it, which is of course, the goal—after all, they're already out with someone else, so to save face, you have to act like it doesn't bother you.

Here are the various options for dealing with this situation:

Go ape-shit on your ex. Let them know every single thing you're feeling and do your best to make them feel guilty, horrible, embarrassed, and sad, all at once. Hold nothing back, including screaming at them, crying, and otherwise making a complete scene. You *totally* won't regret doing this the next day. Also, their new date will question both your ex's choice of past significant others (because you're clearly crazy) and what your ex could have done to piss you off so much.

Go ape-shit on their new date. Step it up. Instead of getting mad at your ex, tell their date how much your ex sucks and every way they ever slighted you. Justify your rant by wanting to warn this new person about what they're getting into. Bonus points are awarded for delivering your message in a calm, controlled voice with a fake smile. If your ex tries to break in and refute anything, put a hand up to their face and keep talking. Again, you *totally* won't regret this after the fact. The fact that you're going to come across as a completely vengeful, petty person is what you want, right?

★ **Pretend like you're super happy and everything is great.** Chances are your ex is just as freaked out as you are about seeing you, so this will throw them. Talk exuberantly about an awesome party you're going to later and about how great work is and how generally *awesome* your life is *now*, (not so) subtly implying that things are much better without your ex. Passive-aggressive, yes, but the next day, you'll be able to live with yourself.

Say hello, pause dramatically, start crying, tearfully apologize, and then leave. Let them explain *that* to their new date.

Be polite but icy cold. Then say something petty and sarcastic, like "Enjoy *that* one," to their date as you walk away.

★ **Be real, but keep your emotions in check.** When the inevitable, somewhat loaded question "How are you?" comes up, say, "I'm doing all right," and return the question. This is honest, but not *too* honest, and therefore won't be super awkward.

Bail on the conversation as soon as possible, and wish them both a good day. After all, despite whatever happened in your relationship with this person that caused it to end, you were with them and liked them at one point. Recognizing that life goes on and finding it in yourself to forgive them (or forgive yourself) and wish them the best is mature and healthy.

▶▶ **You run into your ex and their new significant other somewhere you can't escape, like on a gondola ride up the mountain at a ski resort.**

This is one of those situations that will earn you universal sympathy from friends and foes alike for how totally awkward it is. Run-ins with exes are hard enough, but when you can't escape? And when they're with their new significant other? Torture.

So, how do you handle this? You've got several options:

 ★ **Make it as awful as possible.** You're going to have cocktail party fodder for years from this, so you might as well make it an even better story and escalate the awkwardness. To do so, say things like:

"I'm really sorry again about that little incident. It took me three months to get rid of my . . . situation. Were you able to cure yours?"

"Oh my god, you found someone willing to date you? That's so awesome!! I *told* you you'd find someone willing to put up with that!"

All of this also has the benefit of making your ex super uncomfortable, which can be (let's be honest) vastly satisfying if they caused you any pain. Mature? Not at all. Vindictive? Yep. Crazy? Totally. But won't it be funny to recount later?

Be super (and over-the-top, syrupy sweet) nice. Because your ex is aware of how uncomfortable this is for all of you, being disingenuously, over-the-top nice and complimentary will sound sarcastic and freak them out, but chances are their new significant other will think you're great. This will be annoying to your ex.

★ **Acknowledge the awkwardness (it's honest and friendly), and then talk about something neutral, like the best restaurants in the village.** By far the most mature choice, this will take some willpower. Emotions are bound to be running high, especially if the ex in question is a recent and/or a long-term-relationship ex. Not showing these emotions and being neutral and pleasant will demonstrate your maturity and, in the long run, will probably be the least embarrassing when you calm down later. Unfortunately, it is by far the hardest option to pull off.

▶▶ **You were with your ex for a long time. As a result, your circle of friends overlaps quite a bit, which means that you're now forced into contact with your ex and their new flame on a regular basis (like at mutual friends' parties and group dinners).**

★ **Fake it 'til you make it.** Your only viable option for avoiding an epic cluster of awkward is to be cool and rein in outward displays of what you're feeling. Seeing an ex with someone new sucks and will both hurt and make you feel like hurling, but it's like drinking heavily—the more you expose yourself to it, the less impact it'll have on you, and eventually, seeing them together won't really bother you at all.

If you recognize that you're not ready to be mature and not freak out when you see your ex with his sexy new flame, take some time off from socializing for a while, at least where they're involved. Time heals, so taking a break may make a huge difference. However, take care not to let them control your life by avoiding things you want to do because they'll be there. Not only will you cause a rift in your social circle as people do or don't invite one of you to prevent drama, it's a lot of stress to deal with. Simply coping with it and making sure you're always pleasant will do amazing things for your stress levels, and will also earn you the eternal gratefulness of your group, who are/were probably terrified that your breakup was going to forever alter the friend circle.

You've been looking forward to your small, forty-person, weeklong cruise to Alaska for the past six months—ever since your ex dumped you. To your horror, you discover after setting sail that said ex and their new flame are on board as well. Welcome to your own personal hell.

Compared to being stuck with an ex and their new love for a short period of time (say, on a gondola), a (small) weeklong cruise requires more emotional control if you don't wish to a) ruin your vacation and b) create an awkward clusterfuck of monumental proportions.

Even large cruise ships facilitate repeated run-ins with people, so on a small cruise ship, run-ins are unavoidable and very frequent. And when the huge, muddy, angry elephant that's your previous relationship (and all accompanying break-up drama) is also on board? The potential for being massively uncomfortable is pretty high.

Your options are clear: Ignore them, engage in that fantasy tell-off you've been planning for months, or talk to them and see what you can do about alleviating the epic awkwardness.

Clear the air by getting all your anger off your chest in the form of a ten-minute screaming tirade. The one bonus to releasing that pent-up anger you've been saving for six months on your ex in the spectacular fashion of your fantasies is that you'll probably make things so uncomfortable for them, they'll actively avoid you. However, although you'll have solved your ex-encounter problem, you'll also freak out the other thirty-seven passengers as well. So much for making new friends. **149**

 ★ **Lie and pretend everything is great.** For example, let's say you were planning on ignoring your ex the whole time, but they want to talk to "make sure you're okay." If they push, admit that, yeah, it's awkward that you're all freakishly on board the same tiny Alaskan cruise (because really? You all randomly picked the same tiny cruise? Really?), but you've moved on and are just here to enjoy yourself. Say this convincingly and naturally. As you run into them again and again, pretend they're not there and don't talk to them unless they talk to you.

★ **Suggest a truce.** If you just want to enjoy your damn vacation and not have to deal with it, but you, your ex, and their new significant other all know there's still a lot of undealt-with drama around (because you may or may not have stormed angrily out of the last party at which you were all present, after seeing your ex walk in):

Find them when you're both on deck or at the bar or whatever and acknowledge the awkwardness with a smile. Suggest a truce for the week and emphasize that you don't want any drama—you just want to enjoy your vacation. Basically, let it all go. Don't stress about making friends with them or going out of your way to avoid them—just go about your days and enjoy your vacation. If you see them around, be pleasant. It's likely they'll follow your lead and just go about their business as well.

You've done a good thing by acknowledging the awkwardness, because it broke the ice, and your truce-plea takes away any stress about what may or may not go down while you're all on the boat. This lets you out of any awkward contract that went into effect when you realized you were going to be stuck in close quarters for a week, and is hugely relieving.

Dodge the Awkward Monster

If, despite your plan to let it go, you feel some lingering emotions creep in (like anger, jealousy, sadness, or guilt), find a way to remove yourself from the situation (as in, hang out somewhere away from them for a while, listen to some music, or read a book) and put those emotions in a box until after your vacation.

Then again, you could always kill them and throw their bodies overboard—you always hear about people falling off cruise ships in the middle of the night, right? Just kidding.

(Seriously, don't do that. That was a joke.)

Awkward good-byes: You say good-bye to an acquaintance—someone you've said all you can say to—and it turns out their car is parked in the same direction as yours.

This ranks pretty high on the awkward meter for me. Saying good-bye to an acquaintance can already be awkward—you don't have that much to say to each other to begin with, so ending the conversation was probably fairly abrupt. When you find out they're heading in the same direction as you after saying good-bye, you're faced with either generating more forced conversation or ignoring them, which is awkward because you both know the other is right there. You're not comfortable enough with them to walk in silence, so conversation is a must.

Dodge the Awkward Monster

The easiest way to deal with this is to indicate which direction you're heading in before you actually say good-bye. You know that awkward pause outside the restaurant, when you're both just standing there, waiting to say good-bye? Something like "Well, I'm heading this way . . ." will get them to respond in kind. If they say "Me too" then you can walk with them and say good-bye more naturally once you get to your respective cars. If they say "Oh, I'm headed that way" then you can say good-bye and be done with it, without the fear of them walking in the same direction.

If the deed is done and they're already walking in the same direction as you, you can:

 ★ **Slow down to adjust your shoelace or bag, stop to look in a window, or check your phone, all to let them get ahead of you.** It's far less awkward to be the one walking ten feet behind than ten feet ahead. At this point you can pretend you don't see them or wave and wait for them to pass.

 Pretend you don't see them. Stare at something 180 degrees. Stare down or up. Act oblivious when you can see them waving out of the corner of your eye.

 Run away. Cross the street or pop into a store to avoid having to talk to them again.

★ **Use a distraction.** Talk on your phone to avoid having to talk to them again. Wave as they pass you so they know not to wait for you.

★ **Say, "Hi again," and walk with them.** For conversation starters, try "Where are you headed?" "Do you live nearby?" "Do you come to this part of town often?" "Gee, it looks like it's going to hail frogs, don't you think?" Or continue an earlier discussion.

Awkward waves: You think you're the one being waved at, so you wave back, only to figure out the waver was waving at the person behind you.

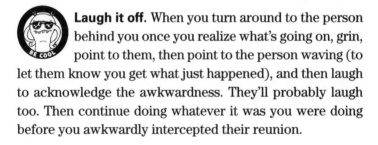

★ **Confuse the waver.** Pretend you were waving back at the person behind them. This has the added bonus of confusing the person behind you as to whether the waver was waving at them or you.

Turn the wave into some arm stretches. After all, that's totally what you were doing the whole time.

Laugh it off. When you turn around to the person behind you once you realize what's going on, grin, point to them, then point to the person waving (to let them know you get what just happened), and then laugh to acknowledge the awkwardness. They'll probably laugh too. Then continue doing whatever it was you were doing before you awkwardly intercepted their reunion.

You see someone you know, make a big deal about waving, and then realize it's not them.

153

★ **Pretend you saw them anyway.** Continue making a big deal (shouting, waving, jumping up and down) and confuse everyone in that general vicinity about whom you're waving at. This will be entertaining to watch and also prolong how long it takes for everyone to figure out you need glasses.

Bonus points for running in the direction you were waving, as if you did see the person you (thought) were waving to and are now going to greet them. Most people watching your antics will lose interest at this point, and you can simply drop the charade and continue with your day.

★ **Confuse them.** There will probably be two or three people looking at you to see who you're waving at, so as soon as you realize you screwed up, act like the imaginary person you were waving at is ignoring you and now you're upset. Flip the imaginary person off. This will cause the people looking at you to wonder who did what to change your attitude from happy to angry. They'll all look at each other with WTF? expressions but won't realize that you made a mistake. They'll either assume you're being crazy or that someone they're not seeing was being a jerk to you. While they're confused, you can blend into the crowd.

▶▶ **An awkward wave has occurred (either you were waving or you intercepted a wave), and now you have to pass by each other. Do you acknowledge anything or just ignore them and keep walking?**

This situation escalates the awkward-wave awkwardness to the next level. Everyone involved knows what happened, but since there's nothing to say, here are some options for alleviating (or ignoring) the awkwardness:

★ **Laugh it off.** Flash a wry smile at them as they pass to let them know you're acknowledging that what just happened was awkward. This is confident and also the most mature way to deal with this.

Ignore them. Bonus points for making a show of doing so, either by rotating your body so that your back is turned to them the whole time they're walking by, or by covering the side of your face closest to them with your hand. They will think you're a freak, but at least you won't have to see their face while they're thinking that.

★ **Pull up your shirt and flash them.** Then say, "Now maybe you'll wave at me next time." Then continue walking as they stand there, openmouthed.

You and your significant other get a little too frisky and break the owner's bed while you're house-sitting.

Oops.

Blame it on anyone but you. If you're feeling shady, you could just pretend that it never happened and then, when the people you were house-sitting for notice, play dumb and say that the bed was intact and fine when you left. Perhaps someone broke in and jumped on the bed? You could also claim that it was that way when you got there and pretend it's their fault.

★ **Confess and apologize.** The obvious stand-up thing to do is to offer to pay for the repairs. Since this can get pretty pricey and is a giant pain in the ass for the people who own the house (because most likely, they'll have to have someone come and pick up the bed to be repaired and then be around for delivery when it's

155

done), in most cases they'll let you off the hook and buy themselves a new bed, making your offer to pay the equivalent of a "No, no, I'll get the check" on a first date. If your fake offer is successful (i.e., they don't take you up on paying for the repairs), send them a nice bottle of scotch with a handwritten apology, and hopefully things will be fine. Just don't expect to get asked to house-sit again.

If your purse-grab doesn't work and instead they say, "Yes, thanks for offering to pay—we'll take you up on that. The estimate for repairs is two thousand dollars," and you can't afford the repairs, you've gotten yourself into one of the most awkward situations around—having to renege on your offer. The very best way to handle this is to be honest about your financial situation and either offer to pay them in installments, with interest, or haggle a bit and see if there's anything else you can do to make it up to them, like free babysitting for the next year.

 You go away on vacation and propose to your girlfriend, at sunset and beachside, something you've talked long and frequently about at work. She says no. You come back to a big congratulations sign made by your uninformed but well-meaning coworkers.

This is awkward because it's humiliating to have to explain what happened and to suffer through the pity, and it's awkward because your coworkers are going to feel like shit for making the sign.

The best and quickest way to deal with the overwhelming all-around awkwardness is to put your emotions aside for a minute and say something like the following:

"Ah, thanks everyone. I really appreciate the support, but unfortunately, she said no. So . . . yeah. I don't want to talk about it—it sucked, but I'm moving on. The best thing for me is to just get back to normal, so I'd appreciate all of your cooperation with that. Better luck next time, you know?"

Then although it will be extremely challenging to walk by all the broken smiles you just wiped off everyone's faces, go to your office and get back to work. Yes, there will be many looks of pity and much speculation immediately afterward and for a few weeks in the future, but by announcing to the group that you don't want to talk and that the thing that will help you the most is forgetting it happened and moving on, hopefully you won't have to have twenty-five grueling conversations reliving the details of your epic rejection.

Remember that your coworkers care about you—they wouldn't have made the sign otherwise—and that any apologies for the sign and other references to your botched homecoming are well meaning. Try to keep your emotions at home and out of the office as best you can, and eventually things will blow over and everyone will move on.

Your friend proposes to his girlfriend in front of a bunch of people, and she says (she's so sorry, but) . . . no.

This situation sucks on several levels. Your buddy just put himself out there and got slapped down like an errant fly on a horse's ass, and now you have to figure out what the F you possibly say to someone who's just been publicly rejected on what was one of the biggest days of his life.

First off, there will be an enormous, all-encompassing, and permeating awkward silence that immediately follows her response as the crowd absorbs what just happened. As a friend, you could jump in and save your buddy at least one half of the double-teamed embarrassment of a) being rejected and b) having a lot of people he knows watch it go down and stare at him to see what he'll do.

157

Take charge. Yell something like "Okay, everyone, let's give them a minute. Everyone out." It will be awkward as everyone shuffles away, but since your buddy is likely to be so shell-shocked it's going to take him a minute to realize he's being stared at and exit the room, you're doing him a favor by having the room bail on him.

It's quite likely that the room would clear out on its own shortly after that, but not after a super-long, incredibly awkward pause where everyone looks at each other (and the couple) and thinks, "Holy shit, did that just happen?" Giving your buddy privacy to figure out what the hell he should say to her "no" is a good-friend move and definitely one to consider.

Make it worse. Jump in on your buddy's private moment and offer to escort the girlfriend to the door (this is unlikely to be received well, however well-meaning it was on your part).

Or, you could ask the question your buddy hasn't recovered enough to ask (and, in the process, put his girlfriend on the spot): "Why?"

Finally, you could yell, "We never liked you anyway!" and lead the crowd out to drink more beer in a show of camaraderie for your (emotionally) fallen buddy.

★ **Leave quietly.** Probably the best way to handle this situation is to quietly leave as soon as the girlfriend gives her answer, grabbing as many people as you can along the way to start the exodus. Once some of the group starts to bail, everyone will follow suit, and you'll have quietly saved your buddy from further public humiliation.

As for what to say to him afterward? A slap on the back, a heartfelt "I'm so sorry," and a stiff drink is the best way to go. In the days and weeks that follow, make sure you're around and available (and that he knows that) for any talking he may need or want to do.

That picture of you doing a keg stand last weekend at the Miller/Peters wedding surfaces on Facebook on Monday morning, and your boss sees it before you have a chance to untag yourself.

The first step in minimizing the damage is to do what you should have done first thing when you accepted the friend request from your boss: Get thee to your privacy settings and limit your boss's access to your account to only what you want them to see (like only pictures you post, instead of those posted by friends). There's always the possibility that your boss saw the picture through someone else's account, but it's important to do what you can to protect yourself from accidental work-suicide via inappropriate-picture viewing.

Assuming your weekend activities in the beer Olympics are not affecting your work productivity, and/or your keg stand wasn't performed while representing your company or in front of clients (assuming that's not what your company is about; if it is, well done!), if your boss confronts you and expresses displeasure, in most cases, it's probably just out of concern that your weekend choices will affect your work. Again, assuming you haven't done something stupid that affects the company or the company's image, there probably aren't grounds to fire you.

Assure your boss that although you understand that the pictures and your partying were ill-advised and you're sorry that they saw you like that, your weekend activities do not and will not affect your work productivity. Remain calm and respectful, listen to what your boss has to say, and make damn sure that, in the future, they can't see any pictures of your raging wedding antics.

If your boss takes the somewhat passive-aggressive approach and "likes" and/or comments on the picture with something potentially sarcastic, like "Impressive" or "Wow," it may be worth touching base to avoid any future awkwardness as a result of this newfound insight into your non-professional activities. Catching them in a non-busy moment and saying something like the following may help assure them that you're still the professional superstar they used to see you as:

"Hey, Bob, I saw that you commented on that picture of me at the Miller/Peters wedding last weekend. I just wanted to let you know that I recognize that the picture and my choice of activity were ill-advised, and it won't happen again. It hasn't affected my work here, nor will it."

Hopefully Bob-the-boss will appreciate your thoughtfulness and understanding of his actual concerns (or your projected fear), and you can move forward with as clean a keg-stand conscience as can be.

Dodge the Awkward Monster

A NOTE ON GENERAL SOCIAL MEDIA ETIQUETTE

* **Don't put your home address on Facebook.**
* **It's generally a not-great idea to preface vacations with posts like "Leaving the house for two whole weeks. Gonna miss you, 72-inch 3D TV! Hope I remembered to lock the back door."**
* **Before you post something questionable, imagine a frenemy gets angry and decides to ruin your life. Will what you're about to post provide fuel? Then don't post it. Duh.**

Guys: You trip at the water cooler and accidentally fling a cup of water onto your female coworker's white shirt, exposing her bright pink bra to the entire office.

However much you may enjoy seeing what color underwear Susie the former swimsuit model has on, it's awkward (and inappropriate) to start an impromptu wet T-shirt contest at work.

Embrace the impropriety. If you're interested in making things infinitely more awkward and potentially getting yourself involved in a sexual harassment lawsuit, you could make a show of staring at her boobs and, as you attempt to "help" by patting down her angrily heaving bosom with whatever cloth is lying around, comment on the color of her underwear: "Nice bra. It's too bad you didn't wear a white skirt—then I could see if I made your panties moist, too." (Bonus points for using two of the grossest words in the English language: *moist* and *panties*.)

★ **Be cool.** If, however, you'd like to get out of this one without ending up in front of your scary HR director and without being a giant douche, direct your eyes at her face only, apologize profusely, grab any available paper towels, and hand them to her so she can soak up the excess moisture. If you've got a jacket or a cardigan on, offer it to her. Offering to dry-clean her shirt is overkill—especially if it was just water—but if you're feeling extra bad, this is a nice gesture. If her shirt is completely soaked, you could offer to act as a human modesty shield as you walk her toward the bathroom, placing yourself between her and prying eyes.

Who knows? Maybe your acts of chivalry will make her see you as a person rather than "that dude in IT," and you'll forever forward be in her inner circle.

Dodge the Awkward Monster

BEST PRACTICES FOR SANE HUMAN BEINGS WHO WANT AS LITTLE DRAMA AS POSSIBLE

✱ Think before you act.

✱ Have safe sex. Duh.

✱ Set parameters at the beginning of relationships. This includes those with roommates.

✱ Don't answer cell phones at funerals.

✱ Honesty is, boringly enough, often the best policy.

✱ Remember when your kindergarten teacher taught you the golden rule? She was on to something there.

✱ When confronted with an unavoidably awkward situation, take a breath or a step back, reassure yourself that this is probably just temporary and your life isn't going to end (yet), and then try to imagine what Mr. Rogers would do.

▶▶ Ladies: You notice that your male boss's fly is down.

What's awkward about this is that you had to have looked at his crotch to notice that his fly was down. He knows that, you know that, and both of you know the other knows. . . .

 Silently communicate with hand signals. You could take the subliminal messaging approach and alternately stare at his crotch and then touch your own fly or smooth down the fabric in front of your own nether regions, although this can go wrong in so many ways. Are you slyly masturbating in front of your boss? Are you hinting that you'd like to have inappropriate relations with your boss? Did your mother not teach you that publicly scratching that region isn't appropriate?

You could also try clearing your throat to get his attention and then pointing to your crotch and making a gesture as if you're pulling up your own fly. There's totally no way *that* could get misinterpreted. . . .

 Adjust his zipper for him. However well meaning you may be, the probability your kindness will be misinterpreted is very high.

★ **Tell him his fly is down.** The best thing to do is to use your words and, while staring at his face (not his crotch), say something like "This is a bit awkward, but your fly is down. I know I'd want to know if it was me."

By acknowledging the elephant in the room (the potential awkwardness), you've actually made the situation *less* awkward—and you've made a longer sentence, which helps prevent the awkward silence that would follow if you had just blurted out, "Your fly is down." He'll say "thanks" and the situation will be fixed.

You just forgot someone's name that you should know.

(As in, you've met them several times—perhaps even hung out with them socially—and you just had a major brain-fade on their name.)

Forgetting someone's name is awkward because it majorly sucks to have your name forgotten—especially if you've run into the name-forgetter several times. If you're the forgetter, it effectively lets the forgotten one know they weren't important enough to merit putting their name in your memory vault. Same goes if you call them the wrong name—it's an emotional slap. Here are some options for getting around all that and hopefully escaping the Awkward Monster as you do so.

(I have an absolutely terrible memory for names, so I have used all of these multiple times.)

★ **Just don't use their name.** If you've run into the person on the street and there's no one you need to introduce them to, just don't use their name. "Hey, how's it going?" works just as well as "Hi, John! How's it going?"

★ **Listen for their name.** If they have a friend with them and introduce you by name as their friend, feel shame and try to catch their name in the ensuing conversation. Then write it down so you don't forget it again.

★ **Wait for them to introduce themselves to your friends.** If you run into them and need to introduce them to your friends, the easiest thing is to pretend to have bad manners and just wait until your friends introduce themselves. Hopefully you'll have seen the nameless person approaching and had time to warn one of your friends that you need help. If not, there's liable to be an awkward pause, but then someone will introduce themselves. You can apologize for not providing an introduction to show that you at least recognize it was awkward that you didn't do this to begin with and (now that you have their name) can gladly explain how you all know each other.

★ **Use generic pronouns instead.** In the super-annoying but thankfully rare case that the name-less person doesn't use their name in the introduction but just says "Hi" or "Hey" or "'Sup," continue on as best you can by using "dude," "you," and/or other generic pronouns to refer to them. Pray that the next time you run into them, they'll be more forthcoming.

★ **Use distraction.** If you forget their name midway through "This is my friend . . .," you could start coughing to cover up the awkward pause until you think of their name—you can even use your finger to indicate that nameless should talk to your friend while you recover—and then listen carefully for nameless's name over your coughing.

★ **Confess.** If no one picks up on your cry for help, and/or if you're feeling mature, confess your forgetfulness, apologize profusely, and ask for their name.

The more socially savvy champion avoiders of awkward know that providing a social smoke screen (humor, distraction) for you both to escape the awkwardness is appreciated—even if the person whose name you forgot knows what you're up to.

So, use levity to escape the awkwardness. Tell a story about how you've been the most forgetful person *ever* today: You even forgot to put in your right contact before you left the house this morning, which has caused you to have to squint like a pirate for the last few hours.

Dodge the Awkward Monster

In the future, enter the person's name in your phone or somewhere else you have easy access to so you remember who they are.

Something Awkward That (Might Have) Happened

>> UNINTENTIONAL WORD SLIPS

It was a particularly crappy Wednesday—you know the ones, where everything goes wrong and you swear that you're paying for being a serial killer in your past life (judging by all the bad luck raining down upon you). I had broken up with the guy I'd been dating the previous week, and my car had died on the way to work so I'd had to walk five blocks wearing heels—in the rain—and in the course of doing so had tripped and skinned my knee, tearing a hole in my best work pants. Then once I got to the office (thirty minutes late), I found out that a very important email I'd sent out the night before had gone to the wrong person (my fault), and the person who was expecting the email had left five (angry) voicemails for me asking where it was. When I tried to resend it, my computer crashed. During lunch, I collided with someone in the coffee shop, and their entire coffee spilled on my shirt. And at around 4:00 PM, my boss yelled at me for something I didn't do. Anyway, by the time I'd finished the day, I was ready to crawl into a hole and never come out.

My coworker offered to drive me home since we lived a couple minutes away from each other. He spent the ten-minute ride telling funny stories about his college years, and by the time he dropped me off, I was laughing—a very welcome change from the rest of my miserable day. I don't know whether it was the crappy day, the funny stories, or just me being tired and used to uttering these three words to friends and family when they'd drop me off, but instead of the "Thanks for the ride, see you tomorrow" I'd meant to say, what came out was "Thanks for the ride. I love you."

I didn't realize immediately what I'd said (as mentioned, it had been a really, *really* long day), so there was a good five seconds of super-awkward silence before I realized what was going on. I apologized profusely and exited as quickly as I could. He was pretty nice about it, (fake) laughing it off, but I could tell he thought it was really weird.

And it was, along with being totally, 110 percent completely awkward. I was so mortified and embarrassed, I very seriously considered calling in sick the next day to get out of having to face him again so soon.

Lucky for me, he acted like nothing had happened, for which I was really grateful.

One would think that an accidental "I love you" to a completely inappropriate person would cure me of the habit, but that wasn't the case. It's happened twice since then: once with a friend and once with another coworker. At times, I define awkward.

Assumptions gone bad: You just congratulated someone on her pregnancy. Unfortunately for you, she's not pregnant.

On the occasions where you haven't obviously checked out her midsection or mentioned a baby bump in any way, you can potentially avoid some major pregnant pauses (ha!) by blaming your mistake on how wonderful she looks, and on your mistaken assumption that this was due to a "pregnancy glow." End with something like "Well, whatever you're doing, it's working. You look fantastic."

If you've made any indication toward a larger-than-normal midsection (through actually mentioning it or via hand gestures), all you can really do in this situation is apologize and move away from the subject as quickly as possible. Further babbling to explain why you thought she was pregnant when she isn't will only dig you a deeper hole: "The way your stomach sticks out really made me think you were with child. Are you sure you're not?"

167

Then once you've escaped your awkward encounter, go home and write five hundred times: "I will never ask about a pregnancy when the person I've spoken to hasn't brought it up first."

▶▶ **You notice that a professional contact you'd like to network with has recently changed her last name, so you congratulate her on her marriage via email as an opening and then segue into a list of the various ways you could work together. It turns out the reason she changed her name is because she just finalized her divorce.**

Apologize and then apologize again. It's an innocent mistake and you meant well, so if you make your apology heartfelt and genuine enough, she should get over it.

In the future, if you're looking to make a personal connection at the beginning of your networking emails, pick something you're sure of, like how her Facebook page says she's on the board of the local cockatoo rescue organization.

Something Awkward That (Might Have) Happened

>> A LESSON IN ASSUMPTIONS

I was on my way to an ugly-Christmas-sweater party with a group of new friends, most of whom I didn't know very well. All of them had known each other for years and so were enjoying that inside-joke, finish-each-other's-sentences thing that close groups of friends enjoy but that outsiders can't really join in. I was nursing a beer, enjoying the laughter, and waiting for us to move on when I noticed another girl who looked like she was with us (judging by the awesomely hideous, red, shapeless, bedazzled sweater covered with snowflakes and yarn pom-poms she was wearing) standing by herself a few feet away. With the intention of making a new friend and having a conversation where I didn't have to ask "Then what happened with the donkey?" to enjoy the punch line, I walked up to her and said the following:

"Wow! You did a great job with the costume! Where'd you manage to find such a hideous sweater for this party? If there's a prize for best ugly sweater tonight, I'm totally voting for you."

Her mouth dropped open, and she gave me a completely bewildered and hurt look and then said, "What party? What do you mean? I'm not wearing a costume."

"Oh. OH! Oh my god. I am so sorry—"

Her, *voice rising in volume and getting higher*: "I can't believe anyone would say something so rude! I love this sweater! I've had it for years and wear it all the time! I sewed these pom-poms on myself!"

Me, *after a pause to contemplate, very briefly, why anyone would voluntarily sew pom-poms on their sweater* : "I am so, so sorry. It's my mistake—I thought you were with our group. Can I buy you a beer to apologize?"

All I got in return was her middle finger in my face and a view of her bedazzled back (complete with flopping pom-poms and matching bedazzled scrunchie!) as she stomped (flounced?) away.

My big mouth and I felt terrible (I can only imagine what it would have felt like to be on the receiving end of my congratulatory insult if I genuinely thought my bedazzling and pom-poms were beautiful—and she clearly did), and I've since sworn to never, ever again assume that someone is wearing a costume unless I'm absolutely, 100 percent sure.

I'll be honest, though—I was jealous of her sweater. I totally would have won the ugly-sweater contest with a gem like that.

169

You inadvertently make someone upset by asking about something painful (that you weren't aware of), like a breakup, the loss of a beloved family pet, or the death of a loved one.

Whether on a first date, mingling at a friend's party, or socializing with clients, this is one of the most awkward social situations you can find yourself in. You feel like an asshole for upsetting someone, and they're forced to explain a situation they'd just as soon not talk about. Plus, it always seems to happen when they've clearly been able to put it out of their mind for a while, and you end up being the jerk who flings it back into the forefront of their life. Go you.

My track record with bringing up recent upsetting things in people's lives is impressive, in a truly awkward way. It happens on a fairly frequent basis, both with people I know and people I've just met. On one of the first dates I had with my now-boyfriend, I brought up the topic of childhood pets and gladly jabbered on about the ridiculous cat I had growing up. When I asked him if he had any special pets in his life, he got very quiet and obviously sad and told me his dog, which he'd had for most of his life, had died . . . last week.

The date ended shortly after that, and I was totally convinced he hated me and was never going to call me again. That didn't end up being the case, but I felt like a completely insensitive jerk for bringing it up.

The only way to really handle this situation is to express heartfelt condolences for the other person's loss, let them talk about it if they seem to want to, and if they don't, change the subject to give them a break. Grief—be it over death, a job ending, or a breakup—affects everyone differently, so your best bet is to be as sensitive as possible to what the sufferer needs or wants. If you really can't tell, it's fine to say something along the lines of "I'm so sorry. I feel so awkward for bringing this up. What can I do to make you feel better?" and go from there.

Another option, after apologizing, is to use some combination of concern and questions that get them talking about their lost loved one in a positive way: "Tell me about [Rover/your great-grandma/your best friend]. What breed was he/Did she live through WWII/When did you guys meet?" Asking "How did he/she die? Was it painful?" is not recommended.

I've been in situations where someone has inadvertently brought up a recent loss in someone else's life, and the conversation turns into a "here's my saddest story" competition. When talking to someone who's dealing with recent pain, this kind of one-upping just seems totally heartless and not helpful at all. However, in other situations, like when the person's loss happened long enough ago that the sting is gone and they're somewhat on their way to accepting it, the stories from other people can end up being humorous in their morbidity, and/or the whole conversation gets so depressing it's funny, which is helpful—laughter can really help bring the conversation back to a happy place.

Managing the awkwardness in this situation seems to be very much a case-by-case kind of thing. There's no right answer for how to handle it, beyond being as sensitive as possible to what the person seems to need.

Something Awkward That (Might Have) Happened

>> DEAR STRAPON.COM, YOU SUCK.

I was browsing gag gifts for a friend's bachelorette during my lunch hour at work. Yes, I know I'm not supposed to be looking at porn at work, but what happened was a total accident. Instead of clicking on the sex-toy store's website, I accidentally clicked on the link to StrapOn.com. What followed was one of the most awkward moments of my life.

To properly relay this story, it's necessary to describe the setup of my desk. I was in the middle of a series of desks—not cubicles, which would have provided slightly more screen privacy—and a main walkway was behind me, giving everyone walking by a full, unobstructed view of whatever was on my screen. Aware of this, I was keeping a close ear out for approaching footsteps so I could switch to another screen and save myself.

I realized my mistaken click as soon as the status bar showed I was being directed to StrapOn.com, and so was frantically trying to close the browser, close the window, stop it from loading, click on something else—anything to prevent what I was sure was going to soon pop up on my screen. Unfortunately, it was a really slow-loading page, and the hourglass of death was doing its slow-motion sand-sprinkling to torture me, disallowing me from clicking on anything else. As a result, I was forced to watch some of the raunchiest porn I've ever seen load slowly on my monitor, in full view of any of my coworkers who cared to walk behind me on their way to the kitchen.

When it was about 75 percent of the way loaded—way more than enough to see what was going on—I heard footsteps. I resumed my frantic clicking, but nothing was happening. In desperation, I turned off my monitor and waited, breath held, to see if the person approaching would notice my noticeably black screen. And wouldn't you know it, the person who walked by was our IT person, who of course noticed—and, naturally, came over to see what was wrong.

Just as he got close, I heard the sound track for the website come on—a mixture of moans, screams, "HARDER!"s, and "DEEPER!"s. I frantically tried to find the volume control for my speakers but must have pushed volume "up" instead of volume "down," because it got really, really loud for a split second before it went silent.

"What was that?" he asked.

I pretended like I hadn't heard anything.

Wrinkling his brow and staring at my blank screen, he said, "Are you having trouble with your computer?"

"Oh no, I was just rebooting."

"Why?" he asked.

"It was just running a little bit slowly," I said. "I thought rebooting might help."

"Do you want me to take a look?"

"Oh, no—it's fine," I said, sweating bullets.

"Are you sure? It's no trouble. Here, let me take a look." I watched in slow-motion horror as he approached my computer, noticed that the power light was still on, and switched on the monitor.

Totally convinced that I was going to have to explain away StrapOn.com, I covered my eyes with my hands as the monitor came to life. When he didn't say anything, I peeked out from between my fingers—miraculously, the computer had followed all of my frantic commands from earlier, and all that was open on the screen now was Task Manager. The IT guy shrugged, set the restart sequence, and got up, giving me and my nervous-sweat-covered brow a weird look as he left.

Never again will I research bachelorette-party gifts at work.

You just got caught looking at something NSFW (Not Safe For Work) at work. Now what? ◀◀

If the computer gods aren't smiling on you and leave your version of StrapOn.com up on your screen for all to see, your options are limited:

★ **Offer an alternative explanation.** Perhaps you made a typo as you were typing, or you got redirected. For example, you could have been

173

doing a search for "cargo straps" as research for your company's upcoming office move, and goshdarnit, StrapOn.com wasn't what you thought it was!

Play dumb. You have absolutely no idea how pictures of bare-breasted women came to be on your work computer screen. None. Someone must be playing a prank on you, because you just went to the bathroom, and when you came back, this site was on your screen.

Confess. Perhaps your boss will forgive you if what you were searching for was embarrassing enough, because after all, searching for strap-on dildos is pretty embarrassing. . . .

Remember to act very contrite, apologize frequently, and blush fiercely. Make sure they know it was for a gag gift. Offer to work an extra hour tonight to make up for your transgression, because you know it was inappropriate, but your internet is out at home and this bachelorette party is next week.

Your boss might forgive you, after a chuckle and glare, but they might also send you to HR for a write-up and a warning about looking at porn during office hours. Hard to tell. It's your gamble.

▶▶ **You mistake a stranger for someone who's wronged you (like someone who slept with you and never called) and then publicly berate the stranger for something they didn't do. When they can get a word in, they tell you their name isn't whatever you said it was.**

Filed jointly under "How to Look Crazy" and "How to Be Awkward," this is a surefire way to provide endless hours of remembered hilarity for your victim and their friends as they relive your tirade, and also to create a one-sided (i.e., your side) hell of awkward for yourself. This is not that awkward for the person on the receiving end of your rant—after all, they didn't do anything. And most people, when they figure out that they're not the intended target of your venom, will be unaffected by your show (other than finding it entertaining).

Once it sinks in that they're not Mike or Molly or whoever you thought they were, here are the options:

Pretend you were just practicing for a play. To make it authentic and get genuine reactions, you couldn't warn them beforehand that it was all pretend. Then ask them how you did and enjoy the ensuing (bound to be interesting) conversation.

Insult this new person. They look like Mike/Molly, and you're already revved up for a shouting match. This new Mike/Molly will make an excellent substitute for your anger. Expect to be escorted from the premises.

★ **Acknowledge your mistake with an "oh" and an "I'm so sorry," and then ask them how you did.** Laugh at yourself and enjoy the potential conversation with a group of fun new people. They'll probably have questions about what Mike/Molly did, which might segue easily into further conversation about how they've gotten screwed over. By laughing at yourself and letting go of the anger (when you figure out it's misdirected), you may well make some new friends (or meet your next Mike/Molly).

Note: This will not work in larger cities, since the person you shouted at will already be running away. Because, let's be honest, publicly berating someone before you're sure who they are is pretty nutty.

You call Friend #1 and immediately start talking trash about Friend #2. It turns out Friend #2 was hanging out with Friend #1 and heard the whole thing because Friend #1 pulled an ultimate fail and answered your call on speakerphone.

You also, in your trash-talk tirade, make references to other similar conversations you've had with Friend #1, further burying both you and Friend #1 in a giant shame hole.

Once you figure out what's going on, you could:

 Hang up. This is an option you don't have when you get caught gossiping in person, so why not take advantage of it when you can? Although it won't get you any closer to resolving the issue, at least it gives you awhile to think about what you've done and how to fix it. Of course, you've just made things even more awkward for Friend #1, since they're sitting with the subject of the gossip, Friend #2, who now knows Friend #1 also talked about them behind their back. Sucks for Friend #1.

When confronted, say you were talking about someone else. Deny that it was the Brittany sitting with Friend #1 you were talking about, and say that you were actually referring to Brittany from work. Pray Friend #2/Brittany believes you.

★ Apologize for talking behind Friend #2's back and talk it out. This may well clear the air and resolve whatever issues you were having. Hopefully Friend #1 and Brittany will resolve their issues as well.

You're Friend #1, i.e. the friend who answered the trash-talking phone call on speakerphone. Now you're face-to-face with Friend #2, the subject of the gossip.

Be prepared for epic levels of awkwardness. Multiply this if the friend who called you references something you know (that you told Friend #2 you didn't know) or an opinion you've baldly stated (when you just baldly stated the opposite to Friend #2). Since you can't bail and lying face-to-face takes way more skill than over the phone, your easiest way out is to apologize and try to resolve the issues by talking them through. Be prepared to deal with some serious hurt feelings—it's a double hit to learn you've been lied to (about what someone said, knows, or thinks about you) and talked about behind your back.

Dodge the Awkward Monster

a. Don't gossip.

b. If you are going to gossip, do a better job of not getting caught.

c. Don't use speakerphone when there's someone else in the room. Duh.

d. If you are going to use speakerphone, prevent any gossip mishaps by cutting in immediately after picking up and saying something like "Brittany is sitting here with me. She says hi."

Guys: You're hanging out with new friends, see a girl, and announce that you're going to "hit that." She turns out to be the wife or girlfriend of another dude at the table.

After the guy in question has pointed out that that's his lady you're talking about, a succinct and sheepish apology like "Oops. Sorry, man. No disrespect meant . . . and well done!" will serve you well, especially when you're sincere about the apology and deliver the complimentary "well done" with a smile.

Most people will find your outburst (and the ensuing awkwardness) entertaining, as long as you move away from it fairly quickly and change the subject (for example, by buying a round of drinks for the table). Dragging things out and making a big deal out of your awkward faux pas (like by apologizing to the lady in question once she arrives at the table: "Hey, I'm really sorry, but I just told all these guys you were smoking hot and I totally wanted to bang you. No disrespect intended") will only make things more awkward for everyone involved.

Dodge the Awkward Monster

In the future, keep your opinions to yourself until all your pals' ladies are accounted for.

You commit an unintentional faux pas, like eating before saying grace or committing a cultural slight at a business function (not bringing a gift, not accepting food offered to you, not finishing everything on your plate, etc.), at a meal with people you can't just laugh it off with—clients, bosses, your girlfriend's family.

If it's something like eating before saying grace, a whispered or mouthed "I'm sorry" to whoever brought you there or whoever is leading the prayer is sufficient. Making a big deal about your apology and/or immediately explaining how your customs are different makes the situation even more awkward. If necessary, you can apologize again to the heads of the household after dinner and in private, with a more lengthy explanation of your behavior if necessary.

If, however, it's a situation where you weren't aware of the custom and have unintentionally offended people (like by not bringing a gift when a gift is brought for you), a sincere apology and a plea of ignorance are your best way out. Show interest in the custom and start a conversation about it (its origins, proper gift selection, their favorite memory of an exchange, etc.) so that it's clear you're respectful and interested in the customs of the people you just offended. Use humor to defuse the situation, including but not limited to acknowledging the awkwardness of the situation and/or relating other (appropriate) awkward situations you've found yourself in. Then the next time you meet this group of people, bring a gift to show you listened and make a joke about not wanting to repeat your mistakes or screw up again.

Most people, when presented with an apology for an unintentional offense and a genuine interest in the custom and culture, will be pleased to educate you and move on. When you show that you learned from your last faux

179

pas by respectfully adhering to the custom the next time, all will be forgiven. Yes, it would have been better not to have screwed up in the first place, but being authentic and sincere about fixing your faux pas will defuse almost any situation.

 ## A friend asks if you're going to a mutual friend's wedding. You weren't invited.

Oops for them. They're placed in the awkward position of being the bearer of potentially hurtful news, and also relaying news that's not especially theirs to relay. Weddings are expensive, so when you (or anyone else) gets left off the guest list, although it feels personal, it was probably a difficult decision on the part of the couple getting married.

There's not much to be said to the bearer-of-bad-news friend, except "I wasn't invited, but have a good time!" Awkward silence will ensue, and the friend will probably say something like "Oh, I was only invited because our parents are friends—I know they had to slash their guest list like crazy," and then someone will change the subject to escape the awkwardness.

As for your non-invitation, if you feel completely hurt, you have some options:

 Send a passive-aggressive gift. Embrace your inner passive-aggressive bitch and send the bride and groom a gift with a note that says "I hope the wedding is beautiful!" Don't talk to them about how upset you are.

 Ask the bride or groom-to-be why you weren't invited and watch them squirm. Maybe you can guilt them into an invitation. Want to be super awkward? This is your best choice. Also, it's a jerk move—planning a wedding is a stress-ball of nightmarish proportions, and dealing with angry and put-out non-invited friends is a sure way for the couple-to-be to feel like crap.

★ **Talk it out**. Buy your soon-to-be-married friend a cup of coffee or a drink and let them know you're bummed you can't be there to celebrate with them on their big day, so you'd like to schedule a raging night out with them (and a few other friends who didn't make the cut) to celebrate their nuptials. This is a pretty rad move on your part, as it lets the couple-to-be (mostly) off the hook and also gives them a fun night out. (And who doesn't like a fun night out?)

You find your neighbor's ferret dead and under the tire of your parked car. You didn't kill it, but it sure looks like you did.

★ **Make it look like someone else did it**. Put the body under the tire of someone else's car and then find your neighbor, express your condolences, and show him the body. Be there for him when he cries over the death of his fuzzy.

Get rid of the evidence. Bury the body and apologize to the karmic gods for wimping out on telling your neighbor his beloved pet is dead. But let's be honest—he's not going to believe you didn't do it if he sees what you saw, and you really can't afford to get kicked out of your rent-controlled apartment if he files a grievance.

Pretend you don't know Mr. Chips is dead. Put the body in a box with an old T-shirt and deliver the ferret back to your neighbor. Tell him you found his sleeping ferret (because ferrets can legitimately look like they're dead when they're sleeping) in a corner of the garage and didn't want him to get hurt, so you're bringing him back up to his apartment. Express shock and horror when your neighbor discovers the ferret is dead. Stick to your story.

Something Awkward That (Might Have) Happened

>> ADVENTURES WITH SUPERGLUE

I had this friend in college (whom I shared a room with) who was a fan of knickknacks, and one of her favorites was this shallow bowl covered in painted flowers she'd found at a flea market. She kept it on top of the dresser we shared and normally used it to hold her keys, spare change, and whatever else she had in her pockets from the day. On this particular day, it was empty and slightly farther over on my side of the dresser than usual, something I hadn't noted but that turned out to be a key component of the next four hours and seventeen minutes of my life.

I had just gotten out of the shower and had managed to put on my favorite knee-high sport socks, some old (granny-panty, super-ugly) underwear (what? It was laundry day), and a T-shirt and was reaching for my pants when I accidentally knocked said dish off the top of the dresser and onto the wood floor, where it immediately broke into four pieces.

I said some bad words and decided that I'd glue it back together for her and beg forgiveness once I'd fixed it. It had already broken twice before (not my fault) in the same places, so I knew it would be easy to repair. I retrieved the superglue and, while sitting on the floor in my undies, proceeded to start righting my accidental wrong. I had just placed the last piece in its place and was holding it together while it dried when my phone rang. I held the dish together in one hand and put my other hand on the floor so that I could stand up . . . except the standing part of that plan didn't happen. I got halfway up and was abruptly stopped when I reached the length of my arm. Surprised, I looked down to see what was going on and realized very quickly that my hand was stuck by my outer three fingers . . . to the floor. I had glued myself to the floor.

Son of a bitch.

Muttering even more bad words, I sat back down, put the stupid (successfully glued) dish down, and tried to see what could be done about my fingers. Twenty minutes—and some serious contemplation of how badly it would hurt if I just pulled hard enough to break free—later, I gave up. My phone was out of reach by about a foot. The nail polish remover, which was the only thing I could think of that might have some effect as a solvent, was taunting me from the top of the dresser, about three feet out of my reach. I knew that my roommate wouldn't be home until just after four, and I'd just heard the local church do its ridiculously long and overly loud gonging that signified we'd hit noon.

Son. Of. A. Bitch.

I tried yelling, I tried grabbing my phone with my toes (which only succeeded in pushing it further away), and eventually, I lay down and waited it out.

When my roommate finally did arrive home, four hours later, I had a striped sunburn on my arm from the open window (and slats—hence the stripes) and would have happily sold my first unborn child for ten seconds with any receptacle that would hold urine. It would have been one thing if it was just her—we could have laughed about the awesome stupidity of me gluing myself to the floor—but

183

she had picked that particular day to bring her four-person (coed) study group home with her so they could put in some hours before their final the next week. The fact that I had a mad crush on one of the guys in her group, who started laughing the second he saw me in all my pantless, flowered underwear/sport-socked glory, just seemed on par with my day thus far.

My roommate, bless her, retrieved the nail polish remover that had been taunting me for the last four hours and set me free, immediately after which I sprinted to the bathroom and had the best pee of my life.

And the dish? In the laughter scuffle that ensued once her study group realized there was a girl wearing no pants glued to the floor, the dish got stepped on and broke again.

I did not offer to glue it back together.

Moral of the story? If you're going to glue something, wear pants. That way, if your crush walks in if and when things go awry, he won't see your laundry-day underwear. Oh, and pee first.

Dodge the Awkward Monster

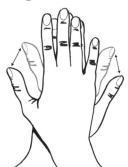

For those of you who don't know (you were probably born before 1985), this is the Awkward Turtle. This gesture, typically brought out immediately after an awkward bomb has dropped and meant to clear the air with a silent "Wow . . . this is awkward," is made by placing one hand on top of the other, sticking one's thumbs outward, and rotating them forward. It's a great get-out-of-jail-free card because if at least one of the onlookers is in the know, they'll laugh!

When downward dog has unexpected results . . .

(page 188)

6

Unfortunately Timed Bodily Functions

When our bodies betray us and go FUBAR at the most inopportune moments, awkwardness ensues. Going #2 and having it not flush, farting during sex, getting your period during yoga—it happens to us all. And let's be honest—bodily functions, however embarrassing and awkward they make our lives, are completely natural parts of being human. The following chapter helps us gracefully handle these little betrayals when they make an unexpected appearance.

You pass gas, audibly, during a meeting. Unfortunately, it's obvious it was you.

★ **The best course of action (and the most mature) is to apologize to the room**: "Excuse me. My apologies," and leave it at that.

Freaking out in embarrassment ("Oh my god!! This is so embarrassing! I'm so sorry, everyone. OhGOD!!" followed by a dramatic exit from the room) or being a jerk in your effort to push blame on someone else when it was obviously you ("Wow! Who did that? Whew!! It reeks in here now!") will likely not be well-received and will just make the entire incident go down in everyone's collective memory as the day you acted like a total drama queen or complete jackass.

Remember that although it sucks just as much as it did in third grade, when you farted during a reading quiz about *Where the Red Fern Grows* and everyone heard it and laughed at you and called you Farty for the next two weeks (I digress . . .), it's ultimately not that big of a deal. Everyone does it. And making a big deal about it and getting outwardly horridly embarrassed (even though that's how you feel on the inside) makes the whole incident much more awkward for everyone, including you.

Something Awkward That (Might Have) Happened

My friend was heavily involved in her university's (mostly female) Spanish club. In addition to the normal stuff—study sessions, cultural events, big dinners and parties and so on—they also offered their non-Spanish services to each other (babysitting each others' kids, helping with résumés and job searches, etc.). Since one member of the group was a yoga teacher, a super-cheap class was available for the club members.

One of the class participants was a nice guy who was really, really awkward: He was a little chubby, he didn't smell great, he was always nervous, and he sucked at talking to the ladies.

Long story short, she told me they were in downward dog in the tiny dark room they used for the yoga class, full of incense and meditative music, and the awkward guy ripped a *big* one. There were only six people in the class, so there was no mistaking who farted.

She said that his slip wouldn't really be a big deal, and she's sure she would've forgotten about it already (given that this all took place about five years ago), but the situation is permanently cemented in her mind because *nobody reacted*. Since this guy was already awkward and uncomfortable in a room full of girls (he was the only guy in the class), his embarrassment was palpable. Had he or anyone else said something funny (or just said *anything*), the tension would have been vastly reduced. She says she regrets to this day that she didn't get up and offer to high-five him to break the tension.

Moral of the story: Sometimes when the situation is beyond awkward, it's much worse to ignore it than just to mention it, break the tension, and move on.

Unfortunately timed bodily functions in bed.

Even in long-term relationships where you've long passed the point of pretending that you don't pass gas, having the urge arrive unexpectedly during sex is not ideal and can range from humorous to horrifically embarrassing and awkward to major mood killer, depending on the length of the relationship, the dynamic between you and your lover(s), and how easily you get embarrassed. I, for one, find this situation to be *totally* embarrassing. I realize that we all do this and it's a very natural part of being human, but logic doesn't help me escape the awkwardness. It still sucks.

189

I blame my above-average embarrassment in such matters squarely on a particularly horrible incident in high school when, during a highly-anticipated first kiss with a boy I liked, I leaned over and accidentally farted loudly enough that it couldn't possibly be mistaken for anything else. Not only was I so embarrassed I cried (which exponentially multiplied my embarrassment level . . .), my humiliation was furthered when *somehow*, all his friends found out and I was known as "that girl who farted" for a good month.

Clearly, crying isn't a helpful reaction when trying to alleviate the potential awkwardness or embarrassment of an unfortunately timed fart—it only draws attention to something that's really not that big of a deal if handled well. Emotions are plenty exposed already when one is naked, so any escalation of any kind is going to make things a thousand times worse.

Dodge the Awkward Monster

Next time, go easy on the cheese plate, take some Gas-X, and put a nice smelling candle in the room to kill two birds with one stone—mask any unwanted smells and create some flickering, romantic candlelight.

In the years since "the girl who farted," I have come to realize that the best way to handle things is as follows:

You know it's coming: If you know you need to pass gas while having relations with your favorite guy or gal, it's common courtesy to excuse yourself for a minute, head to the bathroom (or at least out of the room), do what you need to do, and then come back. This is especially true for any relations involving someone's head below your waist.

Another option: Rather than killing the wave of passion by invoking coitus interruptus to take care of business, it's okay to simply ask your partner to move out of the general vicinity for a second, do your thing, apologize, and then continue. It's not the sexiest situation, but in the moment, the vast majority of us won't care and will appreciate the warning.

It arrives unexpectedly: The only thing you really can do is sincerely apologize (not profusely—this is awkward and draws way too much attention to the situation), and then offer a change of positions to distract them from what just happened. As stated previously, everybody farts, so if it's not a particularly obnoxious one, things may be able to continue as they were.

It's not what you thought it was: In the event that the passing of gas happens to be more than a passing of gas, get thee both to the shower immediately, apologize, and offer a full understanding if your bed-buddy doesn't want to continue. This situation is so incredibly awkward that it may well end up being funny and will go down in your shared history as one of the most memorable moments, recalled with a shudder and an "Oh god, I can't believe that happened" grimace/grin.

There are, of course, other bodily fluids that can make an appearance in bed: vomit, urine, and menstrual blood, to name a few. If it was unintentional (and I pass no judgment for intentional appearances, if that's your thing), all should be handled like more than a passing of gas so as to maintain a hygienic environment in which to romp. However, it should be understood that all of these are natural, very basic bodily functions, and while we have more control over some than others, when we become intimate with each other, although we (typically) don't plan on puking, peeing, or bleeding on each other while having sexual relations, it will occasionally happen and so should be treated with as much levity as possible.

Getting upset, whether you're the person who got puked/vomited/peed/bled/farted on or the one who supplied, is not necessary and will only make things worse. An apology, an understanding partner, and above all, a non-judgmental environment are key for avoiding a mind-boggling level of embarrassment and awkwardness.

 Bleeding in public.

I'm not exactly sure why, but I find situations where I don't know I'm bleeding to be incredibly embarrassing. I'm not talking about serious injuries here—if a shark bites my arm off and I'm bleeding on the beach, believe me, there will be no shame. I'm talking about picking at a zit, a scab, or some other extremely minor situation where a small amount of blood (dried or not) is present, and I'm unaware of it.

For example, I was once waiting for a guy I met online to arrive at the bar where we were scheduled to meet for our first date. I thought I felt something on my cheek—sometimes my hair spray would create a sticky spot, and a hair or a piece of lint or something would get stuck to my face without my knowing—so I pulled whatever it was off (it was a piece of lint, which totally made me feel like a laundry trap), not thinking anything of it. When my date arrived a few minutes later, things quickly took an immediate turn for the date-fail—he responded only in one-word answers and wouldn't look at me. So, a short while later, when I ran out of meaningful questions that, despite my best efforts otherwise, he still managed to answer monosyllabically, I bailed. Once I got to my car, I realized, upon looking in the rearview mirror, that I had a two-inch smear of dried blood on my cheek. As it turns out, I'd nicked myself while pulling the stray lint off my cheek, and it had bled quite a bit. My date hadn't said anything, probably because he assumed I had just finished doing something serial-killer-esque. WTF?

This bleeding-in-public fear is made far worse if no one says anything to alert me to the blood's presence—if they do, I can take care of it, but if I find out three hours later that there is a dried drop of blood dripping down my cheek, I dive straight down the embarrassment spiral, blush furiously, and contemplate moving to a log cabin somewhere in the woods, where I never have to interact in public again.

This reaction alone is super awkward, since it seems that most people don't find this situation quite as awkward as I do. I'm including it here in the hopes that if there's anyone else out there like me, the rest of the population will alert the next person they see that their cheek is leaking and save the leaker the humiliation of walking around all day, blissfully unaware.

Ladies: Unexpected periods and light-colored clothing.

Given my fear of bleeding in public, you'd think this would be a big one for me. Strangely enough, it's not. Don't get me wrong—it still sucks, especially if I'm giving a presentation or in yoga class or at the gym or somewhere else equally public and don't realize what's going on. But it doesn't quite reach the level of awkwardness that unintentional bleeding causes. I think this is because it's something every of-age woman on the planet has to deal with, and any man who has spent a significant amount of time with women will understand.

Hopefully some kind soul will have alerted you to your unexpected arrival, in which case a simple thank-you and a dash to the bathroom are all that's required.

Things get awkward fast when you figure out later on in the day that *no one said anything* and you've been walking around all day with a very obvious indication that you're a woman in heat. Embarrassing? Yes. Awkward? Definitely, especially when you're still around the people who haven't said anything, because once you realize it, they'll know you know that they knew and didn't tell you.

As for how to handle it? Well, unless you realize mid-presentation that your cycle is on display and can do something to hide it, there's not much to be handled except to get your clothing to the washing machine, change, and do a better job of keeping track of when it's okay to wear pastels.

 ## Ladies: Unexpected periods and light-colored couches.

Ouch. Let's just go ahead and up the awkwardness quotient and assume this is your first meeting with your potential mother-in-law or your progress review at work. Pale couch. Red smudge. You. Awkward.

If you get "caught in the act" (so to speak): The best thing to do is to apologize profusely and offer to have the article of furniture professionally cleaned. Most people, recognizing the awkwardness and embarrassment of the situation, will refuse this offer and show you where the spot-cleaning stuff is or deal with it themselves. Crying in embarrassment or showing any other of the various emotions possible (and they range far and wide given the level of awkwardness here) is not advised, as that will just make things worse. A sincere, profuse apology and an offer to clean are ideal, however much you would rather fart loudly in a densely occupied elevator than be there at that particular moment.

If it happens away from prying eyes: Assuming you have time, either have the couch professionally cleaned or spot-clean it yourself (if you're sure of your skills—accidentally ruining the fabric in the process of cleaning would really suck. If needed, explain to the owner of the furniture what happened and what you did to fix it.

Guys: You just noticed that your female coworker has a period spot on her white pants.

You certainly have the option of not saying anything, although this is kind of a douche move, since she'll most definitely want to know and since, if she figures out you knew and didn't tell her, she's going to be insanely embarrassed and/or upset you didn't say anything.

The worst way to handle this is to make a big deal about it. For example, stopping her in a high-traffic area of the office and doing any of the following in a loud voice is probably ill-advised:

1. Laughing at her
2. Asking her if she's dying, because she's got blood on her pants
3. Informing her that you feel obligated as a citizen to report her *Dexter* copycatting to the cops, and then telling her that next time, she should be more careful about blood spatter when she cuts someone up
4. Saying "Well, I guess you're not pregnant"
5. Saying "Ew! Gross!"

★ **Quietly tell her.** Pull her aside and, in a for-her-ears-only voice, let her know she's got something on her pants. She'll get it. If you're feeling extra chivalrous, you could lend her your jacket or sweater to wrap around her waist so the rest of the office doesn't know the intimate details of her menstrual cycle.

★ **Be discreet.** Alternatively, you could pass her a note or alert a female coworker to do the alerting for you, so as to lessen any awkwardness the spotted lady might feel.

She'll be eternally grateful that you were stand-up enough not only to say something, but to do it in an inconspicuous fashion.

You need to go #2 and you're at a crowded house party. Once you do your business, you realize there's a line of people waiting to use the bathroom after you.

It happens. *Everybody Poops*, remember?

If there's a fan in the bathroom, turn it on. If there's a match to light, light it and then flush the match (because let's be honest, setting fire to your host's bathroom trash can would be far more awkward). Wash your hands (besides the obvious hygienic reasons, the soap can also create a fresher scent in the bathroom), and leave the door open a bit when you leave so that the room ventilates.

As for dealing with the person waiting to use the facilities immediately after you, you have a few different options:

 Say something. Let them know they might want to wait a few minutes: "Sorry I ruined the bathroom. [The host] is going to want to get a new one." Or, "You might want to wait a few minutes. I ate some cabbage earlier and . . . well, let's just say I'm all cleared out now." Some consider this a welcome courtesy and will take your twisted humor well. And some find this makes the situation even more awkward—once they walk in, they'll get it.

 Don't say anything. Alternatively, you could just leave them to their own devices. They'll decide what they want to do: hold their breath and go for it, run away, or wait a few minutes.

★ **Blame it on someone else.** You also always have the option of blaming the smell on the person who came before you: "Just so you know, when I went in it kind of reeked. You might want to hold your breath." It's a bit shady, but who's going to know any better?

I'll admit, this last one is my favorite in these situations. Even if the person next in line is well aware I'm the one who made the bathroom smell less than ideal, they're not going to care that I lied and will probably be grateful that I provided both of us with a reason (besides my GI patterns, which they certainly don't want to think about) for why the bathroom isn't Febreeze fresh. Plus, it's always much easier to blame a faceless other party than to know that the person you're talking to is the one responsible.

You've just gone on a (great) date and have headed back to their house for some canoodling. However, you find when you arrive that you need to go #2. You do so, but now the toilet won't flush, or worse, it overflows.

If the toilet won't flush and there's a plunger handy, use it. Many times, this will take care of the problem, and you're good to go, with no one the wiser.

If the toilet starts overflowing, you really have no choice but to yell for the person who lives there. Then, in a show of your home-skills savvy, take the lid off the tank and manually close the rubber stopper valve at the bottom of the tank. This should stop the water from running into the toilet bowl and prevent an overflow if you're quick enough (because, let's face it—having them know you went #2 is far better than having your #2 all over their bathroom floor).

To prevent any further filling of either the tank or the toilet, lift up the float to its highest level and hold it there for a few minutes. The water levels (which are sanitary in the tank, BTW) should return to normal after a bit.* Hopefully by this time, the owner will come in and help you, and the two of you can deal with the problem together (and they'll be extremely grateful that your plumbing savvy saved them a major bacteria-laden mess in their bathroom).

Keep in mind that when a toilet overflows, unless you've done something weird like trying to flush a sweatshirt, it's just that you were the unlucky person to be using the toilet when the system decided to fail. Toilets just don't overflow on a whim—there's usually an existing problem in the plumbing that causes this. So apologize and offer to help, but don't be too embarrassed. It's not all your fault.

Maybe it will even be a bonding experience and a funny thing you can laugh about . . . six months from now when you've gotten over your embarrassment.

 ## You just vomited. Unfortunately, it landed on your date/the bride/your boss/your friend.

Remember the discussion of beer sprayage? Well, this is worse. Whether it's a sudden bout of food poisoning or car or air sickness, or because it turns out it was a bad idea to take six tequila shots in a row, I think it's safe to say that you can tell when the upchuck is coming a few seconds before it actually arrives, hopefully giving you ample time to make it away from others and to get you and your angry stomach to a trash can or bathroom.

 ★ If, by chance, you don't notice the signs and end up hurling on someone, apologize profusely

---

*Google taught me this one, and I've since successfully prevented an overflow. For avoiding the OMG-I-just-overflowed-your-toilet awkward encounter, this maneuver seemed pretty invaluable and therefore merited inclusion. However, I'm not a plumber nor do I have any plumbing expertise, so don't blame me if this doesn't work on your date's fancy European toilet.

and offer to pay for their dry-cleaning bill (and mean it). Most of the time they'll probably be so grossed out that they'll just bail and deal with you later. If they're a close friend or date, do as much as you can to help them clean up (including offering temporary replacement clothes, the use of your shower, and to clean their clothes, if you're able), and then do whatever it takes to distract yourselves until you can laugh about it.

Take any razzing about the incident with a smile, and remember that it happens. If the person you puked on is decent, they'll harass you and move forward. If they're someone you're dating, or just starting to date, hopefully it will end up being a bonding experience. After all, not much is more intimate than viewing the contents of someone's stomach.

You just wet the bed. Unfortunately, you weren't alone when it happened.

As embarrassing and awkward go, this is up there. Maybe you got too drunk, maybe it was a weird dream, maybe you just had an accident. No matter the reason, it's a messy, smelly situation to be in.

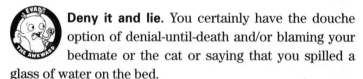 **Deny it and lie.** You certainly have the douche option of denial-until-death and/or blaming your bedmate or the cat or saying that you spilled a glass of water on the bed.

However, if it's obvious you're lying (like the big wet spot is on your side and there is no cat), the best way to handle this is to:

★ Admit it. Do a cannonball into the awkward pool and confess, immediately followed by a major apology and an offer to have the sheets and mattress professionally cleaned. Although it's an incredibly embarrassing (and therefore awkward) confession to make, if handled with honesty and a heartfelt apology, things should blow over eventually—after a large pile of unavoidable harassment from your friend (if you were crashing at their house for the night) or new fling (whom you hope to someday, in several hundred years, be able to look in the eye again), of course. Laughing at said harassment will allow everyone involved to get through it with as little awkwardness as possible.

Dodge the Awkward Monster

In the future, don't drink so much before you fall asleep, or at least make sure there's a puppy in the house to blame.

Note: If the bedding you've just annihilated belongs to someone who has spent any kind of significant time around kids, they will be very used to dealing with unexpected urine. They'll most likely be much more concerned about what sort of medical/emotional situation you have going on that caused you to pee outside the box than they will be about the mess.

▶▶ **You just lost your contact lens in the turkey platter at dinner . . . after your new mother-in-law just spent seven hours making it.**

Biting into a contact lens instead of meat is bound to be weird at best and gross at worst. You've got a couple of different options for how to handle this:

Don't say anything. Of course, when it becomes apparent that you're now legally blind in your left eye because you're missing that contact, your lie of omission will get uncovered, and everyone will wonder why you didn't just say something about losing your contact. Clearly, you're aware it's no longer in your eye.

★ **Lie.** The other, slightly more stand-up, option is to pretend you didn't see it fall into the turkey platter and claim you just lost it somewhere in the vicinity, launching the find-the-contact-lens search we're all familiar with, hopefully involving many people and much hilarity over watching each other comb the ground for the nearly invisible disk. When no one finds it after a few minutes, proceed with dinner and encourage much wine drinking. When someone finds it in their mouth, hopefully their wine-addled brain will find it funny rather than off-putting. . . .

Bladder-control lapses or unexpected diarrhea—in public: Did you just shit your pants?

This just sucks and hits a solid 11 on the 1-to-10 embarrassment scale.

Fortunately, in most cases, mishaps below the belt are usually much, *much* more obvious to you than to the people around you. The accompanying sensations are glaringly obvious to you, but often the visual signals that others might pick up on are actually not all that apparent. A calm walk to the bathroom to clean up, taking care to hold yourself normally and not betray the source of your concern, may well allow the accident to pass unnoticed.

If your accident does get noticed, apologize for any smell and get yourself to the bathroom as quickly as possible to clean up. Maintain your calm. If you wig, the likelihood of others around you getting uncomfortably awkward goes way up. They'll be looking to you to see how you react, so control your reaction, stay calm, deal with the situation, and move on. Hopefully they will too.

Something Awkward
That (Might Have) Happened

>> NOSE EXCRETIONS, BLEMISHES, SPINACH, DROOL, AND INK: THE ATTACK OF THE UNWANTED FACE HITCHHIKER

Let's just say you went to the dentist, and your face is now numb from the eyeballs down. You attempt to eat lunch, but since you can't feel anything at all, this is challenging. You also fail to look in the mirror before you head to a meeting with your boss and coworkers, where you're due to present a project update. End result: You're unaware of the giant smear of mustard coating your chin.

Let's also just say that you're late to your presentation (due to said dentist), so you run in and start talking before anyone has a chance to say anything. When you pause a few minutes later to ask if there are any questions, your coworker tentatively raises a hand and lets you know that you've got something on your face. You reach up and realize you have the better half of a mustard packet happily drying on your chin.

Awkward? Totally—for them and for you. They all want to let you know, because they're good people and would want someone to let them know. But interrupting you in the middle of a presentation to tell you about your new yellow paint job seems much more awkward, because it draws even more attention to your chin hitchhiker, and the possibility exists that perhaps not everyone has seen it yet—something that won't be the case once it's pointed out.

Then let's just say that when you finally do find out, you are so mortified you can't remember your own name, and your obvious embarrassment makes things even more awkward for everyone else, so your coworkers start offering similar stories of when they've had something on their faces to make you feel better. At this point, your now-irritated boss puts a stop to the chatter and tells you to make sure you look in a mirror next time you eat lunch and to get back on track. You could hear a pin drop in the silence that follows.

This happened to me. And it sucked. But it's a perfect example of how our reactions to embarrassing situations make things even more awkward. If instead I had said thanks, grabbed a napkin, and cleaned myself up with a quick explanation of why I looked like a slob (burying my embarrassment and mortification in a box to be opened later that day in the privacy of my apartment), then moved on with the presentation, that five minutes of hell would have been a nonissue and as un-awkward as possible.

Even though it's mortifying to find out you've got a giant piece of spinach covering your front tooth or you've unintentionally drawn a line in marker across your face, obviously getting super embarrassed and dwelling on what happened makes the whole situation awkward when it doesn't need to be.

When space-hogging gets taken to a new level . . .

(page 229)

WTF?

Sometimes we're faced with situations that are so uncomfortable, so embarrassing, and so ridiculous that WTF? is the only reasonable response. Rarely do we know how to handle them, since we come across awkwardness of their caliber very rarely. In order to better prepare us for these awkward bombs, behold the following chapter.

* * *

You find out that your sorority sister is also your future stepmother . . . at Thanksgiving dinner.

Once the shock wears off, take heart in the fact that at least you know what your dad is getting into, and you know you'll get along swimmingly with your stepmom on family vacations. . . .

Be sure to tell an inappropriate story about how she got super drunk and wet the bed her sophomore year, and then let go of your angst and roll with it. Love works in mysterious ways. If your dad is happy? Rock on. The sisters of Zeta are good catches—you would know.

 You loudly quit your job or get in a fight with someone and manage to have the last word, but as you're trying to make your dramatic exit, you realize you've gone the wrong way/you fall/ the door is locked/you push instead of pull and basically end up looking like a giant idiot.

We all wish we had the magical timing of the movies and could pull off a perfect dramatic exit, but in reality, it rarely goes as smoothly as we've pictured in our minds. The last time I had one of these arguments (and successfully had the last word), after my extremely dramatic, front-door-slamming (and satisfying, I'll be honest) exit, I realized I had forgotten my bag, so I had to go back inside and grab that, and then once I got to my car, I realized I had forgotten my car keys, so I had to go back a second time. End result? My dramatic exit (and any effect that may have had or not had) was completely erased, to be replaced with me looking a petty idiot as I repeatedly slammed the door like a crabby child each time I had to grab something and leave again. Oh, and the last time? I had to knock on the door to be let back in (because the person I'd been fighting with locked the door after I'd left). Sigh.

If your dramatic exit goes awry, embarrassment levels will be high, and depending on what preceded your exit (someone wronged you and now feels bad, or you made an angry announcement and bailed), very awkward for those watching your botched attempt to leave.

★ **Make a joke.** If your exit-botching is bad enough (e.g., you slipped and fell or ran into the glass door on your way out and now require first-aid from the person you just walked out on), humor may be your best (and only) way out. It's going to be tough to effectively maintain your "I'm pissed" attitude when you're on the ground and unable to walk by yourself. Laughing at the absurdity and the all-around awkwardness and embarrassment of the situation will get you both through the aftermath as smoothly as possible, hopefully avoiding the worst of the awkward silences that will follow. (After all—what do you really say to someone you just told to F off?)

Make it worse. If you walked the wrong way, pretend not to see the person or people you just raged on looking at you as you walk by them (again). As you head away, turn around and flip them off. Petty? Yes, but definitely potentially satisfying.

Use your failed exit to further make your point. If you were victimized by the push/pull dilemma of glass doors everywhere, continue loudly huffing and/or cussing to further demonstrate how pissed off you are. This is super mature. Not.

You're staying with coupled-up friends for the weekend at their apartment. They keep bickering in front of you. It's awkward.

This is up there among the most awkward situations to be in, because you probably don't have anywhere else to go, and you're at their mercy for things to do.

Ignore the bickering. Pretend everything is fine. When your friend Joe's girlfriend, Diana, says, "I bet you don't say that to your secretary. I'll bet you like it when she makes noise," to his request of "Would you mind keeping it down? I can't hear the TV," laugh and change the subject.

★ **Distract yourself.** Settle in with a book on the couch while they work it out, or try to distract them by suggesting fun things you can all do together . . . like seeing a movie, where no talking is necessary.

Bail. Take yourself on a walking tour of the neighborhood and develop an intense interest in the local coffee shop/bar scene/grocery store.

★ **Talk to your friend.** Say something to the effect of "It sounds like you and Diana are having problems," and offer to snag a hotel room for the weekend. If Joe denies it, embrace ignoring them or distracting yourself for the rest of the weekend.

Get in the middle of things. The next time they have a spat, jump in and say, "It sounds like you guys have some unresolved issues. Joe, did you do something inappropriate with your secretary, or are you just being crazy, Diana?" Let the chaos ensue.

Some jerk almost hits you in the street, and you end up flipping him off. Ten minutes later, your new (highly anticipated and hopefully hugely profitable-for-you) client walks into your office. It's the jerk. And it's clear he realizes who you are.

In order to salvage this professional relationship and cut through the awkward pressure, it's best to treat this with a little bit of humor, no underlying anger, and no accusations or denials. Something like "Ah, my nemesis from the street and I meet again" with a smile and an extended hand should defuse the tension enough that hopefully he'll smile back and return the snark in kind. Once that's passed, you can get down to whatever business you need to attend to.

At a later time and once you've established a good working relationship, use the incident as a way to establish rapport and start a funny conversation. Make sure to exaggerate by saying something like "So, why did you try to kill me the day we first met?"

Your roommate takes it upon themselves to decorate the living room (without your input). You hate it.

You have several options here, ranging from the passive-aggressive to the mature. Here they are, in that order:

 Retaliate silently. One day while they're at work, make the kitchen as hideous as possible. When they ask, pretend that you think it's lovely.

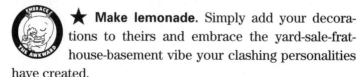 ★ **Make lemonade.** Simply add your decorations to theirs and embrace the yard-sale-frat-house-basement vibe your clashing personalities have created.

209

Pull a crazy. One day while they're busy, take down all their decorations and pile them in the middle of their room. Then put up all your stuff.

 Suggest a compromise. If they take down their black velvet portrait of Elvis, you'll stop tonguing their milk carton.

 ★ **Talk to them.** Explain that while you appreciate their life-size posters of still-frames from seventies porn, your grandmother may have a heart attack the next time she comes over. Is it possible for them to project their personality in their bedroom only, keeping the living room a neutral zone?

▶▶ **Your roommate is a giant slob but doesn't acknowledge it, even after you point out that you can no longer see the couch or coffee table under all their stuff.**

Your passive-aggressive plan of (what you feel is conspicuously) leaving their mess and cleaning up yours isn't working because their mess threshold is way higher than yours. Basically, their mess just ends up driving you crazy and leaving them unaffected. And since you pointed out that perhaps it would be a good idea if you both worked harder on keeping the living room clean (and by both of you, you meant them), the situation has gotten worse—their crap is so thick on the coffee table that you can't even see the Ikea wood laminate anymore.

Plus, to your great dismay, last Thursday they commented on how "clean" the living room looked after you cleaned up your stuff and left theirs in a pile in the corner. &*#%!!

★ **Hire a housekeeper.** Slap them with half the bill at the end of the month. You'll have your sanity back, even if they think you're crazy.

Get passive-aggressive. Start making a pile of their stuff in the middle of their room whenever you clean up (as opposed to the corner of the living room). It's not your job, but if they won't listen, this will at least keep you sane. They probably won't like this, but it will prove a (totally immature) point about how much of their stuff is out and about in the apartment.

Make an ultimatum. Tell them you're moving out unless they can start keeping their stuff clean, or if you're the one on the lease, tell them they have to start doing their share of the cleaning or you're kicking them out. This is harsh and will make you look like a mess-tyrant, but fear of being forced to move could potentially be effective in scaring them into cleaning up. Be prepared to deal with the loss of a friend.

If you're going to take this route, figure out exactly what you want from them, and then sit them down and tell them you've got something serious to talk about: "I like you and want to keep living with you, but I just don't think I can take the mess anymore. So, I realize this sounds intense, but here's my deal: Unless you can start making a bigger effort to keep the living room and kitchen clean, I need to move out [or I need you to move out], because the current situation just isn't working anymore."

★ **Talk to them.** Talk to them again and tell them you really need them to make more of an effort to clean up their stuff. Point out that nothing has changed since the last time you asked.

211

"So, I brought the cleaning situation up before, but nothing has really changed since then and—I'll be honest—it's driving me crazy. I really like you and want to keep living with you, but unless this mess situation resolves itself, I don't think I can stay here. Do you think we can talk about finding a solution for this that we're both happy with?"

 You've been hooking up with your roommate for the last year but just broke it off. Now you're living with your ex.

You were the one who decided to live on the wild side and shit where you eat, so unfortunately, this is part of the deal until you can escape your self-made-hell lease. Hopefully one of you has a friend's couch to crash on until a better living situation is figured out, but if not, here are a few ground rules for avoiding the worst of the awkwardness.

* **Be nice.** Agree to put any passive-aggressive or petty BS aside until you're able to find a new living situation. Breakups blow to begin with, and being forced into the same vicinity as your ex on a daily basis is going to blow even more. Add any extra drama to that, and you've got a major war on your hands. Be prepared for it to be hard, and agree to be polite and nice to each other, despite the anger, resentment, sadness, guilt, and/or hate you may be feeling. If it's easier, agree to only talk if it's necessary, like about shower scheduling.
* **Schedule alone time.** If you really can't stand being around each other, work out a schedule for when each of you will be there. Chances are you both have friends you can crash with a couple days a week, so figure out a compromise so that at least two nights a week each of you gets some alone time in the apartment.

* **Agree not to bring any new conquests to the shared apartment.** If you are going to F the pain away with someone new, do it at the new person's house. The situation is hard enough to handle without throwing your new activities in your ex's face.

* **Find reasons to not be at home.** There's nothing more depressing than living in a space you used to share with an ex. Until you can rearrange and redecorate to wipe the memories (assuming you're staying and they're going), or until you can move out, this nonstop reminder would drive anyone crazy. So develop an obsession with yoga classes, writing in coffee shops, or watching feel-better-about-myself-by-watching-the-trainwrecks-on-reality-TV with your friend at their house.

Your roommate's boyfriend, after using the bathroom in the middle of the night, comes into your room instead of your roommate's room. You discover the mistake in the morning.

 ★ **Oops.** Perhaps it was just an honest mistake on both your parts: Maybe you were asleep and rolled with the addition of a warm body to your bed, and maybe he was just confused as to the layout of the apartment. Although it's a hard pill to swallow, after you, the errant boyfriend, and your roommate discover what happened in the morning and have the inevitable talk about the "Oops," your roommate should eventually get over it. As long as nothing happened (nothing happened, right?), it's a no-harm-no-foul situation that you'll hopefully all be able to laugh about in the near future.

You're the jerk. You noticed he was there but pretended to be asleep so you could enjoy her boyfriend for the night. If this was the case and you want your roommate to speak to you again and continue being your roommate, you're better off lying and claiming it was an honest mistake.

He's the jerk. He noticed you weren't his girlfriend but went with it because he thought you were hot. You really were asleep and didn't notice until morning. This is creepy, and if he admits his foul, it's time for a heart-to-heart with your roommate, strongly advising against her continuing the relationship and/or allowing him to come over anymore (and if he does continue to come over, install a lock on your door). However, the only person who can say what actually happened is him (i.e., he's the only one who really knows whether or not he knew what he was doing), and if he's a creepy but smart dude, he'll claim it was an honest mistake, and you won't have any ground to stand on. Install a lock on your bedroom door and watch your back.

Make lemonade. Neither of you noticed until morning, making it an honest-mistake kind of situation. But now that both you and your roommate have snuggled with her boyfriend, why not take things to the next level and suggest a threesome?

▶▶ **Your significant other's best friend just hit on you.**

Besides it being awkward because every time you see the friend in the future this will forever be between you, now you're in the unfortunate position of having to figure out whether or not you're going to tell your significant other.

＊ **If you do tell**: At the very least, mad drama between your S.O. and their friend will ensue. So might the end of their friendship—and that's assuming everyone is honest about what happened. If their friend lies and tells your significant other that *you* were the one to hit on *them* (out of retaliation for you rejecting their advances, for example), you've just created a shitstorm of awkward and potentially the end of your relationship, if it gets bad enough.

✳ **If you don't tell:** If you keep quiet and your girl-/boyfriend finds out later from another source that their friend hit on you, questions will be raised about why you didn't say anything to begin with—are you into their friend and that's why you didn't say anything? What else are you hiding?

Yikes.

The first order of business, before you even consider the to-rat-them-out-or-not question is to shut down the advances. Let's assume it all goes down at a party you and your S.O. have thrown at your apartment.

Make a scene. One (not particularly mature, but effective) route to take here is to make a scene so that your S.O., along with everyone else, will find out what just happened. When you receive the invitation from the best friend to "get out of here and check out my place, wink wink, nudge nudge," respond immediately and as loudly as you can with "I can't believe you just asked me that. Do you care about [insert your S.O.'s name here] at all? I would never, ever do that to them, so no—I will not have sex with you."

Even if people missed the first part, by the time you finish, the party will be silent and everyone will hear with great clarity the "I will not have sex with you" part of your tirade. You've now just successfully placed the conniving friend in a position of extreme awkwardness by calling them out publicly. Even if they try to act like you were

215

the one hitting on them, you said it first, so you're the one that people will believe, especially if you treat the friend's response with crossed arms, angry eyes, and disappointed facial expressions.

 ★ **Use an unsaid threat.** If scenes are not your thing, a firm and angry response of "Not in a million years. And you're a two-faced, awful beast for suggesting that," followed by a disappointed shaking of your head and walking away, should let the friend know, in no uncertain terms, that they've been rejected. Walking away will leave them in fear of whether or not you're going to tell, which is good. Of course, now you're faced with whether to tell or not, but at least you've made it clear to the friend that they're a jerk.

As for the to-rat-them-out-or-not question, in general, being honest and communicative is a better bet than not.

Of course, all of the above assumes that you didn't and don't want to accept the advances of the best friend. If you do want to accept said advances? Do the right thing and break up with your S.O. first—even though hooking up with their best friend after you've dumped them is rough, it's more evil to cheat on them with their best friend.

If you've already cheated? Go lie in the bed you made, you ass, and say good-bye to your relationship. Generally speaking, cheating on your S.O. with their best friend is an unforgivable offense.

▶▶ **You just found out you have to work with your ex's new girl-/boyfriend.**

 ★ The obvious mature reaction is to have a conversation with this person and explain your connection to them. This ensures you're both aware and can be somewhat cautious of each other's feelings and avoid obvious hot spots—like their new relationship with your ex. Be polite to them and professional, and put any jealousy, anger, hurt, or vindictiveness in a sealed box, never to be spilled on them.

Yes, it will be hard and will probably suck, but hopefully you'll get to know them as someone other than "your ex's new girl-/boyfriend," and any negative feelings will fade away on both sides.

After all, it's just as awkward for them—no one likes their new flame's ex. The ex is almost always a perceived threat, even if things are totally dead between the new flame and the ex, and knowing that you—the ex—are walking around with (very) intimate knowledge of their girl-/boyfriend is going to suck for them.

If you don't feel like being mature, other options for handling this situation include:

 Make your working environment so bad for them, they leave. Make it clear you don't like them and never will, both to them and to everyone else you work with. This makes every encounter you have with them extremely uncomfortable and puts your coworkers in an awkward position every time they need to decide whom to eat lunch or do a project with. Who doesn't love more drama in the workplace? Bring it.

Be a homewrecker. Befriend them without explaining your connection to them, and then encourage them to break up with your ex. "Enemies closer," right? Plus, this way you can remotely get back at your ex for breaking up with you. Surely no bad karma will haunt you for this.

Be passive-aggressively bitchy. Do things like saying hi to everyone else but them when you walk into a room, throwing away any food they put in the communal fridge, and "forgetting" to include them on company-wide emails so they're at a disadvantage. This totally won't come back to you in the form of an HR warning or worse.

▶▶ **Over the water cooler, the passive-aggressive twit you work with just managed to rather skillfully pay you a back-handed compliment: "OMG, I love that color on you! Wait . . . is that the same shirt that the girl who just got fired for her revealing clothing had? I think it might be. Huh."**

Unless you're a professional comedian or a sitcom writer, chances are good you're not going to have a pithy comment to respond with, such as "So funny you should say that! The nineties called me this morning, and they said they really want your shoes back."

The thing about this one is that they started it, so you have control over how awkward it gets. And in a case where you suspect someone is trying to be a jerk without actually coming out and being a jerk, escalating the awkwardness, although juvenile, is a pretty decent response if you can't come up with anything suitably scathing in return.

Also, if it turns out they were actually trying to pay you a compliment and you just took it the wrong way, the following will save your bacon and prevent you from looking like an asshole when they were just trying to be nice.

Let's examine:

Your coworker clearly has no other motive than to be a bitch by saying to you, "The girl who just got fired for her revealing clothing had that shirt," but her passive-aggressive delivery clearly puts her in the "I hate conflict" camp. Clearly, your only possible response is to throw it back at her and make her really uncomfortable:

Her: "The girl who just got fired for her revealing clothing had that shirt."

You: "Oh. So, did you mean that as a warning to me or something? Do you think what I'm wearing is too revealing?"

Her, *clearly lying*: "Um, no. I'm just saying she had that same shirt."

You: "Well, clearly you're observant about what I'm wearing. Do you like me or something? I've got to tell you, you're not really my type, and honestly, this conversation is making me uncomfortable. According to HR rules, you need to back off."

Her: "What? What are you talking about? I'm not hitting on you."

You: "Then why did you make a comment about my clothing? I find this really inappropriate, and I'd like you to stop."

Her: "Dude, you are so off base. I don't like you like that. Chill out."

You: "Look, it's pretty clear to me that you wouldn't have said anything if you weren't checking me out, especially since you already told me it wasn't to warn me that my clothing is too revealing—which also supports my point that you're checking me out, by the way. What other reason could you have for talking to me about my clothing choices that way if not to let me know you were looking?"

Her: "Um . . ."

You: "Exactly. I'm just letting you know ahead of time that if you approach me again I'm going to HR. I've already told you your advances make me uncomfortable and I'm not interested."

Her, *looking at you like you're crazy*: "Sorry. Whatever you say."

Win.

When someone insults you, but they say it as a fact.

The following happened recently to a friend of mine:

He was meeting his girlfriend Jenny's grandparents for the first time, and when Jenny introduced him to her grandmother, her grandmother smiled at him and said, very politely, "Jenny! He's much fatter than you described."

My friend wanted to know how the F to handle this.

 Reply in kind, in an equally polite voice. Try one of the following:

* "Jenny! You didn't tell me your grandmother had no social filter, you naughty girl, you!"
* "Funny! I was about to say the same thing to Jenny about you!"
* "My belly's not the only thing on me that's huge. . . ."

 Scold her: "Well, that's not very nice! Don't they teach manners to octogenarians anymore?"

★ **Acknowledge the insult, then move on.** "Ouch! She's a firecracker, this one!"

In general, insults hurled directly at you are best handled by hurling the barb right back at the hurler, not getting upset (this only encourages and is satisfying to whoever was rude enough to insult you to your face), and then moving on. Dwelling on something coming from someone that rude and bitchy isn't worth it.

You just got caught being a jerk (or you caught someone random being a jerk to you), like pushing the door-close button when someone clearly wants you to hold the elevator.

>> THEY'RE THE JERK.

 ★ **Ask them why they did it.** A fun option for making things even more awkward, they'll either a) deny it, b) get really embarrassed and mutter some excuse, or c) get angry and accuse you of lying.

Get passive-aggressive on their ass. Push all the buttons to antagonize them. It's worth keeping in mind that anyone who's mad enough to hit the close button on an approaching would-be elevator rider may get a bit aggro at you for being that annoying.

Let it go. Ignore them. Be boring.

>> YOU'RE THE JERK.

★ **Lie and tell them you didn't see them.** You could thwart the awkwardness by lying and saying you didn't see them, even if it's obvious to you both that you did, in fact, see them. This is an acceptable white lie in society, used to avoid an extremely awkward fifteen seconds (or so) of looking everywhere but at them (the ceiling, the floor, your bag, your shoes, the buttons, the safety information above the buttons) while they shoot daggers at your back. Your lie will probably go uncontested, unless they've also read this book and turn the first situation back on you. At that point, you can make a new friend by asking them if they've read *Awkward*, and the two of you can bond over your similar (and awesome) literary choices.

 Apologize. Another option is to apologize for being a jerk and say you're having a bad day (because presumably you are—who pushes the door-close button when they see someone coming on a good day?). This leaves very little room for follow-up conversation and will mollify your fellow elevator rider(s).

Get crazy. Finally, there's always the option of passive-aggressively letting the person know how irritating it is that they got in *your* elevator by sighing loudly when they get in and shooting death glares at them for the duration of the ride. Then as you get off, be sure to mutter something like "asshole" under your breath. You can continue on your merry way knowing they'll be deliciously mystified at your obvious misanthropic tendencies.

▶▶ **Awkwardness on airplanes.**

Airplanes occupy their own universe of awkwardness. Where else are you squished next to (potentially totally weird/disrespectful/freaky) people for hours at a time, and does getting up at the wrong time run you the risk of getting Tased by a trigger-happy air marshal?

Tensions generally run high when you stuff 150 strangers into close quarters (turning nice, reasonable adults into crazy people with barely-contained air-rage), so communication can occasionally be a challenge.

Because of the sheer number of awkward/annoying things you can do on an airplane (that will cause any number of awkward altercations and conversations with your fellow travelers), it seemed more efficient to list all the potential offenses first, since they all basically get handled the same way (which is explained after the list).

So, in the interest of promoting air-peace everywhere, here are twenty-nine totally awkwardness-inducing things we should all avoid doing on an airplane. Pick any of the below if you want to get in a fight and/or annoy the shit out of those around you.

* **Paint your nails.** Or remove your nail polish with nail polish remover.
* **Spray perfume or put on heavily scented lotion.** I know it's not your fault that some of us have freaky allergies, but me going anaphylactic next to you on an airplane because you sprayed mango-scented perfume into the *recycled air* is not going to make your flight a peaceful one. I will freak out and look like I have a highly communicable disease once I swell up, break out in hives, and stop breathing. You will be scared.
* **Bring on any smelly food, such as a tuna-fish sandwich that's been warming in your bag for the last four hours.** Because that's just mean. Same goes if you brought something delectable, because for those of us who didn't think of buying In-N-Out Burger before we boarded, it makes the plane a hellish torture chamber filled with the mouthwatering scent of greasy hamburgers. Jerk.
* **Chew with your mouth open.** Seriously, it's way grosser when I can't move away from you.
* **Fall asleep on your neighbor's shoulder**—when you don't know them. Bonus points for drooling.
* **Hog the armrests.** Pick one. Stick to it. Give the middle seat a break and allow them to have their armrests.

* **Sneak-read your neighbor's magazine/book/Kindle/iPad/computer screen.** Ask questions about what you see.

* **Use the seat in front of you to pull yourself up when you go to the bathroom.** This will give the person in front of you mild whiplash whenever their seat bounces back into place. This will suck for them.

* **Repeatedly move things into and out of the seat pocket.** Or open and close your tray for no apparent reason, making sure you let it fall down and bounce each time you release the latch. To the person in front of you, this feels like being kicked repeatedly in the kidneys.

* **Hum out loud along with your iPod.** This is especially awesome if you're off-key.

* **Sing.**

* **Practice for your poetry slam, loudly.**

* **Bounce in your seat.** This may cause my drink, which was sitting on my tray table, to deposit itself on my neighbor, which will be entirely your fault. I will blame you.

* **Pass gas, audibly.** If you must do the deed, apologize. This goes a long way toward keeping the peace. Next time, try to make it silent—then at least there's a plausible chance that it was one of the other 149 people.

* **Have a make-out session with your neighbor.** Or try to round the bases when you're two of three people sitting in a row of seats.

* **Ignore the "don't talk to me signals" your neighbor is giving you.** These might include putting their headphones in, looking super interested in their book, or closing their eyes. Talk to them anyway.

* **Flail or otherwise cause your drink and/or food to end up on your neighbor.**

* **Step in dog poo before you board, complain loudly about it, and then deny that it's you.**
* **Fail to sedate your terrified pet before boarding.** Not only do I feel terrible for your cat/Chihuahua having to be stuffed under the seat in front of you in its ridiculously small carrier, but hearing it meow/bark, hiss, and cry are heartbreaking and grating all at the same time.
* **Wake up your sleeping neighbor to ask them if they want your extra pretzels.**
* **Puke.** If you get airsick (or drank too much) and feel the need to vomit, please attempt to do so in the vomit bag provided, or get yourself to the bathroom. I feel bad for you, but if you puke on me, I will puke right back on you. Also, I'm fairly sure this will cause a negative feedback loop of puking for us, so really, it's in your interest to puke elsewhere.
* **Do anything private, like popping a zit, picking your nose, or using nail clippers to trim your nails.** Your invisibility spell isn't working—everyone can see you. There's a teensy-tiny bathroom. Use it.
* **Invade your neighbor's space.** If you are larger than a ten-year-old girl and don't fit comfortably in the seats provided, a simple acknowledgment and apology for any bumping or invasion of personal space that may occur is very appreciated. We're all stuck here together for a while, and being polite does wonders for defusing air rage.
* **Get up, sit down. Repeat.** If you're a frequent urinator and for some reason have chosen the window or middle seat, ask the aisle seat occupant if they wouldn't mind switching. They will probably say yes so that they don't have to get up every ten minutes and be forced to become intimately aware of your bladder functions.

225

WTF? <<<<<<<

* **Hit on your neighbor, repeatedly.**
* **Stare at your neighbor.**
* **Touch yourself.** And yeah, I'm talking about *that* kind of touching. Even if it's through your clothes, it's pretty obvious what's going on. Again, there's a teensy-tiny bathroom. Go there, if you must.
* **Find subtle ways to touch your neighbor.** This is super creepy if they don't know you and have not made any sort of indication that they're into joining the mile-high club.
* **Let your child bite, kick, hit, or scream in your neighbor's ear.** Seriously. Not cool. We're all aware that we're not allowed to bite, kick, hit, or scream back, but believe me—we're thinking about it.

Handling the offenders: On airplanes, communication, although sometimes harder to muster than passive-aggressiveness, is the way to go. So, if you're on the receiving end of any of the previously mentioned twenty-nine annoying things to do on an airplane, the ideal way to handle it is through the following:

1. **Take a deep breath to calm down.** Do this both in the interest of keeping the interaction pleasant and so that you don't go ape-shit and get Tased.
2. **Once you're composed, politely ask the offender to stop whatever they're doing that's bothering you.** For example, "Excuse me, but would you mind not using my seat to pull yourself up? When you let go, it bounces and is hurting my neck. I'd really appreciate your help on this."
3. **Repeat,** if necessary.
4. **Quietly tell on them.** If your neighbor continues their annoying behavior after two attempts

to talk to them, go find a flight attendant and quietly (and somewhat anonymously) complain. S/He'll come and address the situation.

5. **Obviously tell on them.** If it still continues, you now have some pretty solid ground to stand on when you push your call button and narc on the offender to the flight attendant. It's a lot harder to be rightfully annoyed if you haven't said anything.

The cold hard reality is that some people simply suck. If there's room on the plane, you can ask to move to another seat, far away from your sucky seatmate. More often than not, however, you're stuck and have to deal with it. Such is the plight of modern air travel.

For example, I actually had a guy say no to me when I asked if he could get up so I could go to the bathroom. I was in the middle seat, and it was hour four of a six-hour flight— and for the record, this was my (and my window neighbor's) first time asking him to move. Baffled, I didn't know what to say. The window neighbor tried asking—same response: "No." I waited a couple minutes and then decided to ask again: "Maybe later" was the response. My window neighbor finally called the flight attendant over, and the attendant asked the guy to move. His response to us? "Why didn't you just say something? There's no need to have the authority figures intervene."

WTF?

>> OOPS. I'M THE ANNOYING ONE

If, on the other hand, you're the one doing anything on the above list, and you realize you've screwed up, an apology and/or an acknowledgment that you know your behavior has been/is annoying is a great first step. Follow that up with a promise that you'll try to stop (or, if you can't stop—as would be the case if you keep bumping into the offended because your neighbor keeps pushing into you—that you're sorry), and you'll be well along the road to helping to make everyone's time together more pleasant.

>> BUT I'M NOT DOING ANYTHING . . .

If someone asks you to stop doing something, regardless of whether or not you think you're doing it, be polite and try to address the situation. If they're just being crazy, enlist the help of the flight attendant. They're pros at smoothing over ruffled feathers.

 How to handle the kid who won't stop kicking your seat on an airplane.

There comes a point:

* after you've talked to the parents a couple times and asked them nicely to discipline the child who's bruising your kidneys or making your eardrums bleed with their screaming,
* after you've asked the flight attendant to say something—perhaps more than once—and,
* after you've tried and failed at your yoga breathing

. . . that the situation becomes so out-of-control that losing it seems like the only viable option.

After all, screaming at the four-year-old behind you to shut the fuck up and stop kicking your seat is totally reasonable. Not.

Unfortunately, yelling at someone else's kid not only sets you up to get into a majorly awkward situation with the parents (who, BTW, will be understandably on the kid's side, you air-raged kid-yeller, you)—you're stuck next to these people for the next few hours, after all—but it will also probably cause the kid to kick harder, scream louder, or otherwise increase the frequency and sound of whatever it was they were doing to begin with (and if you freak out on their kid, this behavior may well be encouraged).

Plus, think about the parents. Do you think they love knowing that their child is actively disturbing someone else, or a couple hundred someone elses? No. No, they do not. Traveling with children is no easy task—for anyone involved. Sometimes taking a moment to remember this can help.

★ **Ignore the kid.** My best advice is to pre-purchase some noise-canceling headphones before you get on your next flight and to Zen out as best you can. If you pretend hard enough, perhaps the kicking could feel like one of those mechanized massage chairs.

Something Awkward That (Might Have) Happened

>> CREEPY LURKERS: AN OPEN LETTER TO SEAT 6E, ON A FLIGHT IN OCTOBER 2010

I had the window, the flight was full, and there was a dude next to me. He either had deceptively large shoulders and didn't fit into his allotted space (he didn't appear to be that big of a guy), or maybe the guy on the aisle kept invading his space, forcing him to invade mine. Whatever the case, this is what happened:

I fell asleep shortly after takeoff, with my head leaning against the window. Awhile later, I woke up and found that the guy was RIGHTTHERE, as in, his head was about five inches from my face, with his arm resting entirely on our shared armrest and his upper body leaning over the armrest and into me. He was reading a book, which was less creepy than if he'd been looking down my shirt or something, but it was still a major invasion of my space. I tapped

229

him on the shoulder nearest to me and asked if he wouldn't mind moving back into his seat. He looked up from his book, looked around, apologized, and then moved his body back into his seat area.

Weirded out, I tried to read for a while but eventually fell asleep again (I'm kind of narcoleptic on airplanes). When I woke up, I again found most of his upper body in my space. We're not talking about a simple lean toward the window, as you might accidentally do when resting your arm on the armrest. We're talking about over-the-top leaning, as your significant other might do when resting their head on your shoulder—except he wasn't actually touching me; he was about an inch away from doing so. I jumped when I opened my eyes and saw him, and this time, I wasn't quite as polite and pushed him away when I asked him to move, again. He didn't apologize, just leaned back into his seat and continued reading.

I considered pushing the flight attendant button and complaining but found that I didn't have the balls. I'd have to explain what happened right in front of him if I did that. I could only imagine the level of awkwardness. And what would the flight attendant say—"Sir, please try to stay in your space?" Plus, we were already descending and no one was allowed to get up, anyway. So, I tried to squish myself as far away from him as I could against the outside of the plane and prayed that the rest of the flight would go quickly.

So 6E, thank you for totally creeping me out.

 ## Gift exchanges with new significant others.

Birthdays, anniversaries, and holidays can turn into hugely awkward hot messes in new relationships.

What if you started going out in November, and by mid-December you totally dig this person and want to get them something to show your affection but don't want to freak them out by going over the top? And what if they get you something far more thought-out and nice than you get them? What if they hate what you get them because you don't know each other that well yet? OMFG.

If you both didn't have the foresight to talk about a gift exchange and determine some ground rules (how much to spend, whether to do it at all), handling gift exchange mishaps merely requires an ability to laugh it off, no matter how much you feel like going home and sobbing in the shower.

For example, you decide to get her diamond earrings, and she buys you a DVD.

Her: "Oh my god. You got me diamond earrings. You *really* shouldn't have. Really. We've only been going out a month . . . that's only four weeks." (*Note the lack of an exclamation point and the emphasis on "really" in "really shouldn't have."*)

You: "Oh."

To defuse this awkward bomb of too-much-too-fast affection:

 Tell her they're fake. When she loses one, hide your horror.

Guilt her. Ask her why she doesn't care about you as much as you obviously care about her. Then say "Just kidding! LOL!" Enjoy the now-even-more-awkward silence. Hopefully she'll laugh.

★ **Freak her out.** Tell her, in a serious voice, that apparently it was a good thing you didn't decide to propose. Keep up the seriousness until she looks like she's super uncomfortable, and then wink at her to get her to laugh.

231

⭐ **Tell the truth.** Say that you thought they were beautiful and so is she, and although, yeah, maybe it's a little over-the-top, you really like her and are excited to see where this relationship goes.

⭐ **Laugh (so you don't cry).** For example, "Whoo-eeee, this is awkward. I guess we should talk about gift plans next time, huh?" Then laugh. Hopefully she'll join in.

▶▶ **Awkward first dates: You meet some of your date's friends, and they say something to you like "Well, let's hope you don't make her as crazy as the last one."**

WTF are you supposed to say to that? What does it mean? What did "the last one" do that made her crazy, if anything? WTF.

Try to make her crazy to see what her friends are talking about. Call her by names that aren't hers and then pretend you didn't. Don't call (but pretend you did) and then accuse her of not remembering to call you back. Answer her reasonable, nonthreatening questions of "So, what did you do today?" with "Someone's nosy," and/or "I didn't hang out with any other girls, if that's what you're asking." Once you push her far enough, hopefully she'll do whatever it was that made her friends say that. At least then you'll know what you're getting into. The problem is that she's going to bail on you after you treat her like that, so there will be nothing to get into.

232

Ask her if she's crazy. Tell her the reason you're asking is because her friends told you she was. This will cause major drama, so you'll see what she's like under pressure. You may destroy her relationships with her friends (and her relationship with you, since that's not exactly what her friends said) in the process, but again—at least you'll know what brand of crazy she is under stress.

 Ignore her friends. If and when the crazy ever comes out, you can kick yourself for not listening to them. Until then, you can call *them* crazy.

 ★ **Have the ex conversation with her and find out her side of what happened.** If she tells you she took an axe to his truck, it may be time to cut your losses and bail.

The Facebook unfriend: The modern, passive-aggressive "F you."

>> SITUATION 1: How to deal with someone confronting you about unfriending them.

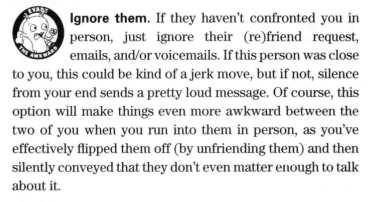 **Ignore them.** If they haven't confronted you in person, just ignore their (re)friend request, emails, and/or voicemails. If this person was close to you, this could be kind of a jerk move, but if not, silence from your end sends a pretty loud message. Of course, this option will make things even more awkward between the two of you when you run into them in person, as you've effectively flipped them off (by unfriending them) and then silently conveyed that they don't even matter enough to talk about it.

 It's obviously Facebook's fault that you're not showing up as their friend anymore. This excuse (adjusted for provider) can work for not returning voicemails, texts, and emails, too. This is definitely the doormat way out, but if you're too much of a pansy to stand behind your passive-aggressive "F you," this is a good option. Then again, it doesn't really get you anywhere if they push to refriend you. It also puts you in the unfortunate position of having to keep lying to them

"Nope, I totally didn't get your friend request."

"I tried sending a friend request to you last week, but I guess it didn't go through. Crazy, right?"

"I totally clicked accept, but you're still not showing up. That is *so weird*."

★ **(Re)friend them. Then do what everyone else does and hide them from showing up on your feed.** Now you get the benefit of not having to ever think about them, but none of the fallout from an unfriend confrontation. Again, if you don't want to deal with explaining why you don't like them anymore, this is a wussy, albeit effective, way out.

Tell the truth. You don't like them anymore. You found out they slept with your bestie and never called her again. You went on one date with them two years ago, and you're culling your friend list to people you actually talk to.

Whatever it is, you obviously have a reason for unfriending them, so be honest. The reason may be harsh and may well create a totally awkward silence afterward—after all, you just broke the long-standing social norm of avoiding talking about how you actually feel. But in the end, being upfront and honest leaves no one in the dark about what's going on and could end up being beneficial: at least they won't ever bug you on Facebook (or in real life) again.

>> SITUATION 2: How to confront someone about unfriending you on Facebook (or when someone won't accept a friend request).

It takes a concerted effort to actually unfriend someone on Facebook, so chances are good it's not a random mistake, especially if you actually know this person. If you don't know them that well—like you had a drunken make-out session at a party six months ago and haven't ever talked again—you may just be the victim of a friend-list culling session.

★ **Send them a (re)friend request.** The least confrontational way to get yourself back in their good graces (if you feel that you've been unfriended wrongly) is to send them another friend request, with a (short, friendly, non-whiny, non-desperate) message explaining who you are and your connection to them ("We made out at Jane's party") and asking if they want to meet up for coffee or something to establish the relationship further than just on Facebook. No reply? Move on, or continue escalating the confrontation with the following plan.

Email, Facebook message, or call them and say you're sure it's Facebook's fault that they're no longer showing up on your friend feed and that your friend request didn't go through (damn technology!), so would they mind refriending you? This is totally passive-aggressive, and they'll see right through it, but you've backed them nicely into a corner where the only ways out are to be really socially awkward and tell you the truth (they don't remember you) or to use your conveniently provided excuse (Facebook screwed up) and refriend you.

Email, Facebook message, call, or face-to-face confront them (whatever it takes to get an answer) and ask straight up why they unfriended you. This isn't awkward at all. Or psycho. Nope.

Because you're forcing them to explain their problem to your face (which is way harder to do than through the once-removed-from-reality land of the interwebs), you'll create an exponentially more awkward situation for yourself. If you're in the game to mess with this person and make them squirm a bit, this is a great option.

▶▶ **How to handle acquaintances (and others with whom awkward silence sinks in after two minutes maximum of conversation) and repeated run-ins (e.g., at a concert, at a restaurant, while browsing in a bookstore).**

I think repeated run-ins with people when you've already maxed-out conversation are among the most awkward encounters out there. I've been in a bookstore with acquaintances of this sort and have (embarrassingly) actively hidden from them to avoid further one-word, super-awkward exchanges.

These are the people that we're not really friends with and probably never will be, but because we both know we know each other, it's awkward *not* to say something to them. However, after something like the following, the thought of forcing more small talk makes eating spiders sound appealing (no offense if that's your thing, but I accidentally almost ate a large spider once, and it's not an experience I'd like to ever repeat . . . or succeed at).

For example, while in a bookstore:

Me: "Hey . . . you! How's it going?" (*Note the "you"—99 percent of the time I've also forgotten their name, which adds a nice second layer of awkward.*)

Acquaintance: "Hey! It's good. Good to see you."

Me: "You too. So . . ."

Acquaintance: "So . . . what're you here for?"

Me: "Oh, I'm seeing if I can find something good for a friend for their birthday. Have any recommendations on new fiction?"

Acquaintance: "Um, let me think. Um . . . not really. The last thing I read was that vampire meets zombie meets mammoth shark book."

Me: "Gotcha. So . . . what are you looking for?" (*They asked me, so it's only fair to ask them.*)

Acquaintance: "Um, I'm just kind of browsing."

Me: "Cool. Well, um . . . see you around. Have a good day!"

Acquaintance: "You too. 'Bye!"

We part ways, breathing twin sighs of relief. Five minutes later, we bump into each other in the self-help section.

Me: "Ha! Fancy meeting you here."

Acquaintance: "Haha! Yep . . ."

Me, *debating whether or not to ask what they're looking for, but that just seems really awkward in the self-help section, and the eye contact is getting super uncomfortable, so I pretend the cover of the book in front of me is super interesting*: ". . ."

Acquaintance, *focusing on their nails*: ". . ."

Me: "Okay, see you later."

Acquaintance: "K. 'Bye!"

Repeat at regular intervals until one of us leaves the bookstore (or hides).

So, how do you handle this?

★ **Hide effectively.** This could involve sitting in the magazine section and intently browsing through a magazine. If someone looks really involved in what they're reading, the other person is off the hook for having to talk to them again.

Or you could play squirrel and keep them always just out of sight on the other side of a shelf. (You know how squirrels always hide on the opposite side of the tree trunk when you walk by, moving so that the tree is always between them and you? Like that.)

Or you could ask for help from an employee—this occupies you enough that you won't have to talk to them if you run into each other. All that would be necessary is a passing smile.

 After the third or fourth time, say something not funny, like "Are you following me?" This will make things just awkward enough that conversation isn't necessary, only a smile.

 Use your cell phone as a prop and focus on that every time you see them. Same philosophy as focusing on a book or magazine, but unlike a book, you can carry around your cell phone as your get-out-of-awkward-free card without having Loss Prevention stalk you through the store.

 Bail. Effective, but annoying if you actually had a purpose in the store.

▶▶ **Someone just cut in front of you in line, and you correct them by tapping them on the shoulder and politely letting them know the back of the line is behind you. Instead of apologizing, they ignore you or get angry and say something rude.**

The problem with this one is that anyone brazen enough to thwart societal constructs (like lines) is probably not easily reasoned with, so your options for actually rectifying the situation are pretty much limited to ratting the perpetrator out to the manager of the store. The other issue is that the perpetrator probably doesn't care that they've upset you, annoyed you, or pissed you off. This leaves you with the choice of a) making things exponentially more awkward or b) letting it go.

Obviously the latter option is boring (albeit the mature thing to do), so I'll focus on the former. Here are some suggestions for upping the ante and making the line cutter regret having picked you to cut in front of.

Passive-aggressively harass them. Sigh loudly, "accidentally" bump into them as you "accidentally" drop something (to give you a reason to bump), stand just a little bit too close, breath or cough on them, or mutter insults you're too chicken to say to their face. All of these are great for potentially annoying the line cutter, although I make no promises you won't get arrested for harassment.

Talk loudly about them. Call your bestie on your cell phone and/or talk loudly to the person behind you for the next ten minutes, complaining at top volume about the jerk wearing the red jacket who just cut in line.

Start singing eighties rock ballads, Jimmy Buffett, or show tunes loudly. This is an almost guaranteed way to annoy the hell out of not only the line cutter, but everyone else in line as well—and as a bonus, you may be asked to leave the store.

▶▶ Unreturned confessions of love: You bravely decide to attempt a push from the Land-O-Friend to Romance Island with your best friend. They say no.

You were sure they were going to reply to your declaration of "I love you" and attempted kiss with open arms, lots of tongue, and an enthusiastic reply in the same vein. Unfortunately, what you got was a super-awkward push away and an "I'm really sorry, but I don't feel that way. I think we're better as friends."

Now things are weird. And awkward. Here's how to get them back (as close) to normal (as possible).

Step 1: Be honest. Be honest with yourself and with your friend. Do you need some time away from them to get over them? Do you need to talk it out? Can you let go of the dream of the two of you together and enjoy as much of their company as they can give you?

Step 2: Act normal. Once you're recovered enough to continue with the friendship (if that's what you choose), it's your job (as the instigator of your friendship pot-stirring) to set the vibe for fun and to make every effort to act normally. Make it clear you're ready to continue on as buddies and that this won't affect your friendship—as this is what they (and probably you) are most afraid of.

Remember that if you act weird, your friend is going to act weird, too. It's challenging for them to know what to say to make you feel better. As your best friend, they love you and don't want to see you hurt, especially by their hand, so they feel bad for hurting you and guilty for not feeling the same way. The first time you see them after your three-word bomb will be very anxiety-ridden for them as well. If you show them through a smile, a hug, and a "We're all good" that you meant it when you said this wouldn't affect your friendship, they'll feel a million times better.

Not being weird includes not getting outwardly upset about them dating someone new—best friendships are special because you can talk to each other about everything. Striking relationship woes off the list of talkable items is a pretty major change, so if you want to be in this person's life and be there for them, you need to put your jealousy aside and be a friend.

If you find you can't handle it? Learn how to deal, either by asking them not to talk about their new flings or by pulling back from the friendship until you *can* handle it. If you ask for the former, expect that the relationship will change and some walls will go up—when we have to watch what we say, we become more guarded.

Step 3: Move on. You don't have to ignore the sadness of losing what could have been with your bestie, but you do need to make an effort to get through it. Because your dreams of what could have been have just been dumped on, this can feel like both a rejection and a breakup. So, if your bestie can support you, as they would in the event of any other rejection or breakup, all the better. You'll be closer to them for it.

Your best friend just attempted a move from the Land-O-Friend to more. You aren't feeling it. Similar to if you were the one initiating the move to more, how you react plays a huge part in how awkward this ends up being.

Presumably, the decision on behalf of your friend to move things into romance territory was not made lightly—after all, the stakes are high. If you don't return their feelings, it's awkward at best and the end of the friendship at worst. That's scary.

Since they're probably pretty freaked out about how you might react (now that it's clear you're not interested in them that way), as someone who cares about them, control your freaking and, when you're ready to speak, remain calm, using humor to lighten the mood if possible:

"Wow. [*Smile.*] I'm very flattered that you think me worthy of liking that way, but I'm really sorry—I just don't feel that way for you. I can't even imagine how much courage that took, and again, I'm sorry for not being able to reciprocate. You're my best friend, and I don't want that to change. Friends?"

Then in the following hours, days, weeks, and months, act normally. Your friend may need some time to get over the hurt of not getting what they wanted—if that's the case, support them just as you would if they were going through anything else. If you need some time to process what happened, communicate that to them and then take that time. Keep the conversation going so that there's little chance of miscommunication, and eventually the relationship will settle back into itself.

The biggest things to remember when you and your bestie have a threesome with the Awkward Monster are: be honest with yourself about your feelings, be respectful of your friend and their feelings, and above all, remain calm and supportive of each other. Do that, and the Awkward Monster will waddle on his merry way.

▶▶ **Someone bumps into you (really hard) in a crowded bar, which pushes you into someone else, which causes them to spill their drink all over. They get pissed, get in your face, and tell you that you owe them a drink. You disagree.**

If you're a confrontation-avoider, this one is super awkward (even if for the confrontation-comfortable, it probably doesn't even register).

Dodge the Awkward Monster

FOR THE EXTREMELY SHY

Confrontation (and dealing with other people confronting you) gets easier with practice. Until it becomes easy to handle, simply pretend that you're someone else for a few minutes. It's easier to jump out of our comfort zones and do something we're scared of if we're not "us" when we do it. So pretend you're acting a part in a play or channel your best friend (who has no problem with confrontations), and put all your doubts, fears, and anxiety away for a few minutes.

★ **Out-awkward them.** Look the high-maintenance twit in the face, pause for dramatic effect, and then say, "No." Then either walk away or stay put, but stay silent and ignore them. Silence, a highly underrated tool (for everyone, but especially for the more shy) in these situations, is extremely useful here, as it's very difficult to argue or prove a point when the other person won't acknowledge you.

Of course, if high-maintenance has anger issues, you may end up getting pushed or punched, in which case you can file assault charges.*

Deflect the blame. Say, "Nope, *they* owe you a drink," and point to the person who pushed you to begin with. This aligns you with high-maintenance (so they can do the confronting and you won't have to), and the two of you can ask for new drinks together.

★ **Inject some Zen.** Say, "I'm sorry your drink spilled, but someone pushed me into you. Losing a

---

*Again, I'm not a lawyer—but I think you'd win this one.

drink kind of goes with the territory when it's this crowded, so why don't we just all move on and enjoy our nights?" This is mature and reasonable, but there's no guarantee that high-maintenance will be reasonable, so you'll just have to see what happens. If they continue freaking out, you can just walk away.

Dodge the Awkward Monster

In general, successful confrontation-handling involves staying calm and (therefore) keeping your emotions in check, whether those are anger, fear, or embarrassment. Remaining logical and objective, listening to whatever the other person is saying, trying to figure out why they're so irate, and then acknowledging whatever it is that's frustrating them will make them feel heard and hopefully defuse the situation. Letting emotion rule and/or not listening to the other side will only escalate the energy of the interaction, therefore making it more uncomfortable and awkward. And if you can stay calm in the face of someone screaming at you, you're always going to have a better handle on the situation than they are.

▶▶ **Your great-auntie Claire just asked you at Thanksgiving dinner what happened to that "nice girl" you were dating last year, right in front of your new girlfriend.**

After you've recovered from choking on the stuffing you inhaled in shock and horror when the question hit your ears, calmly tell Auntie Claire that things didn't work out with the other girl and that now you're with [insert new girl-friend's name here] and are very happy.

Turn and smile at your girlfriend lovingly so she knows you're being sincere, and then change the topic and ask

Auntie Claire about her favorite subject—how much she won at the blackjack tables the last time she was in Vegas.

Something Awkward That (Might Have) Happened

>> FUN WITH LUBE

I was at a sporting goods store looking for that anti-chafing stuff that comes in a stick to prevent rubbing while running, except I was experiencing major brain-fade on what it was actually called. This is what followed:

Me: "Hi. Do you guys have any of that lube you use while running? You know, the stuff you rub on your nipples?"

Clerk: "What . . . ? I just . . . what? I think you might be in the wrong store. You should try that sex store across the street."

Me: "What? No. It's the lube you use when you're exercising. You know, to prevent chafing from repetitive motion and fabric and stuff? I'd be surprised if you guys don't have it."

Clerk, *staring at me like I'm crazy*: "Oooooookay. Let me ask someone else. [*Gets on the loudspeaker.*] COULD ANYONE WHO KNOWS WHERE TO FIND THE LUBE PLEASE CALL DESK FOUR? THANK YOU." *Snickers echo throughout the aisles.*

Me, *blushing furiously*: "Was that really necessary? You made it sound like sexual lube. I want the kind for running."

Clerk, *staring at a point above my head*: "Look, no judgment about your personal life, but I really think you have the wrong store."

Me: "Oh my god! It's the anti-chafing stuff! It comes in a stick like deodorant, and you rub it on yourself to prevent chafing."

Clerk: "Oh! You mean the anti-chafing running sticks. Why didn't you just say so?"

245

Over the loudspeaker: "DESK FOUR, WE ARE UN-ABLE TO LOCATE THE LUBE. PLEASE GIVE OUR APOLOGIES TO THE CUSTOMER. [*Snicker.*]"

Me, *rolling my eyes*: "Yes. That's what I said. The anti-chafing stuff. Do you have it or not?"

Clerk: "Actually, that's not what you said. You said 'lube' and something about nipples."

Me: "Ugh! Whatever. Do you have it?"

Clerk, *with a smug smile*: "Yeah. It's in aisle seven, next to the bug spray."

Me, *trying to keep my face from catching fire from blushing so hard*: "Fine, thanks."

Clerk, *over the loudspeaker*: "LUBE SUCCESFULLY LOCATED. IT'S IN AISLE SEVEN." *More snickering follows me down the aisle, to the cash registers, and out the door.*

I haven't been back to that store since.

8

Seriously Awkward

Sometimes the situations we find ourselves in are so awkward and so uncomfortable—and not in an embarrassing way, but more in a this-cannot-be-seriously-happening-right-now way—that the normal tricks for escaping or evading the awkward (running away, using humor to lighten the situation, being a passive-aggressive jackass) just won't work. Our only option is to deal with these straight up.

You catch someone you know in the act of doing something shady, like stealing money from your wallet. They deny that's what they were doing.

As it turns out, it's really frustrating to try and communicate with someone who won't admit they were doing anything wrong.

There is a certain breed of manipulator who is great at getting away with all kinds of wrongdoing, despite getting caught. They're very skilled at turning the tables and making the situation about you (the confronter) treating them (the victim) badly and at focusing on your thinking the worst of them. Even if it's completely clear to you what they were doing (as in, what possible legitimate reason could they have for taking $40 out of your wallet and putting it in their pocket, when you haven't given them permission to do so?), they'll have an excuse ready and they'll stick to it. (They were borrowing money, and they guess you aren't the person they thought you were if you aren't okay with them doing that. Don't you trust them?) The very, very best manipulators will make you feel like an ass for saying anything and will have you apologizing to them at the end of the discussion.

To avoid this tomfoolery, stand your ground. After you do your confronting and deliver your "What the F are you doing?" just let them talk. Stay silent. Keep your back straight, your chin up, and your arms crossed as you stare steadily at them. Avoid slouching, crossing your feet, and having shifty eyes—these all convey weakness, and you need to look strong.

★ **Silence is golden.** Silence, as well as a steady gaze, works wonders for making even the most accomplished manipulator nervous and also gives them nothing to feed off of. Let them get angry, sad, or frazzled, whatever—just focus on maintaining your stoicism. Be non-reactive and at the end, when they've run out of steam, just say something like "Give the money back, and don't ever do that again" (or whatever you want the outcome to be), and show them the door (or back to the party or away from your jacket and/or purse). If you don't handle confrontation well, this is a great way to handle things.

Even if they're not an accomplished manipulator, silence and steadiness are really intimidating to almost anyone who gets caught doing something wrong. The situation becomes awkward for them, not you, and chances are good they won't mess with you again.

Reacting to everything they say and acknowledging a potential excuse drags you into the fray and into the awkwardness, and makes the whole thing way worse than it needs to be. When dealing with someone who denies what's happened (they've been caught) with excuse after excuse, it's difficult to have a productive, reasonable conversation.

A friend confesses their love to you while drunk one night and insinuates that, unless you reciprocate, they're going to hurt themselves.

Emotional blackmail coupled with the not-to-ever-be-taken-lightly threat of bodily self-harm? It doesn't get much more awkward than that. Your first responsibility upon hearing that someone wants to hurt themselves (or is thinking about hurting themselves or has mentioned hurting themselves) is to get them some help. There are multiple suicide and mental-health hotlines whose contact information is readily available with quick fingers on Google. You can also simply dial 911 if you think the threat is imminent.

If the threat is not imminent, I strongly recommend consulting a professional psychologist about to handle this or any other situation where someone has threatened self-harm. I am not a professional psychologist, but that said, I think it's important to remain true to your own feelings and to not bow to the person's demands—in other words, dating them to protect them from themselves isn't a viable option. It's also worth remembering that if they're trying this kind of manipulation on you, their emotional issues are quite clearly bigger than how much they think they love you. Since they're a friend and you care about them, do what you can to get them help, but don't lead them on or be dishonest in the name of protecting them.

 ## Your significant other just proposed. You don't want to say yes.

Marriage is a big deal. When the person who loves you takes a huge chance, opens their heart, and tells you they want to spend the rest of their lives with you, this bravery and this love should absolutely not ever be taken lightly.

So, if you realize you can't, in good conscience, say yes—no matter how much it may hurt your significant other to hear you reject them and no matter how scared you are of how things may change in the future because of this—it's vital to remain true to your feelings. By doing so, you respect the person more than if you say yes and then have to renege at a much more awkward date, like once the wedding has been planned.

So return that bravery that they laid out for you, and be honest.

You just asked an offhand question (like why your new friend doesn't like to go shopping), expecting that the answer will be lighthearted. Their answer ends up being very serious and intense (like they fought off a would-be rapist in a department store, and so now they hate shopping).

This is awkward because not only were you not prepared for a serious answer, but also what can you possibly say that will properly express your empathy for their obvious pain? You don't know this person well enough to know how they like to be supported, but they wouldn't have said anything if they didn't want to you know, so what do you do?

Your best (and honestly only) course of action is to let them know you heard them and that you're recognizing that they're sharing something big. Do this by stopping what you're doing (whether that be walking, doing the dishes, checking your email, etc.) and turning to face them. Take their hands or place your hands on their arms, and then express your heartfelt condolences: "I am so sorry. That must have been terrifying for you."

Then listen.

They wouldn't have brought it up if they didn't want to talk, so let them talk. Actively listen to them and focus on them—it is tremendously satisfying to be *heard* when we speak, so do them that service.

The awkwardness will very quickly pass once you're settled into the conversation, so let it run its course and then move on by suggesting a change of scenery, some food, or a drink.

You got a little drunk last night and slept with your friend's ex. And to make matters worse, you realize you like the ex.

A step up from kissing your friend's crush, sleeping with your friend's ex is a tough one for a friendship to get through. Knowing that your ex is sleeping with other people again is never an easy pill to swallow, but when one of those other people is someone who's supposed to be on your side? Ouch. That said, this person is your friend's *ex*, which means that although it's a tough situation, everyone is an adult and should hopefully be able to deal with it.

If you care about your friendship and respect your friend, you need to say something. They're going to find out eventually, and it's going to be far easier for them to hear the news directly from you than if they hear it through Tracy, who talked to Robin, who heard from John that you banged Lisa's Andrew last week.

So call Lisa and ask to buy her a cup of coffee because you have something you need to tell her. This will set the tone for something more serious, which will allow her to put up some emotional defenses ahead of time and not be quite so vulnerable. Once you have her in front of you, lean toward her, face her fully (both of these are body-language indicators that you care about her and want to talk), and say:

"Lisa, this is really hard, but I did something last night that is going to hurt you when I tell you. I wanted to be the one to tell you rather than having you hear it later on from someone else, both so you know how sorry I am for hurting you and so that you know the whole story."

Then tell her what happened. Leave out the sordid details (natch—your aim is to torture her with this information as little as possible), but be honest. Was it a one-night stand? Do you like Andrew as more than just a F-buddy? Will it happen again?

Your point in telling her is so she knows what's going on and can process it and so that the two of you can have some prayer of keeping your friendship going.

If it wasn't just a one-night stand, you have to tell her you have feelings for her ex. This fling could turn into something more serious, and if that happens, you're all going to have to deal with it. It's a tough reality that an ex finding love with a friend of his former flame isn't all that unlikely. After all, his ex's friends are her friends because they're similar people. And if our friend's ex loved our friend, it's quite possible that he might find a connection with one of her friends as well. If ultimately that connection turns serious and makes you (her friend) happy, it's unlikely your friend will stand in your way. She may need some time and a lot of talking to work through it, but she loved him once, too, and probably wants him to find happiness as well. If he finds it with you? It's rough, but at least she'll know you're both good people.

Something Awkward That (Might Have) Happened

>> STEP 1: HOLD FOOT. STEP 2: INSERT IN MOUTH.

This is going to make me look like a horrid bitch, but it's one of the most awkward things I've ever gotten myself into, so here it is—my worst moment:

> I was shopping in a large department store, one of the ones where the sales staff checks on you every few minutes to see if you need a different size. The girl helping me was really nice and very attentive, so when I was having trouble finding a particular style of dress, I asked her for her advice.
>
> She brought me some suggestions, and eventually I noticed that the dress she was wearing was exactly

253

what I was looking for. She said she'd grab me one and bring it in and asked me what size I wanted.

Now, here comes the awkward part. What I was trying to say with my answer was that I, in a completely objectively and non-bitchy, non-snarky way, had observed that she was roughly one to two sizes bigger than me. So, just as you would size up how big someone's water bottle was or how many pounds of potatoes you wanted by judging how big or small someone else's bag o' potatoes was, I asked her what size she was. She told me, and then—without thinking (and I still kick myself for not using my brain and my will-this-sound-awful-or-not filter before opening my big and tactless mouth)—I said:

"Oh, okay. I think I'm probably a size smaller than that."

MEEE-OW and ouch, right? As soon as the words were out of my mouth, I realized how horrible and mean it had sounded and fell all over myself apologizing to her. I tried to explain what I had meant—which naturally ended up with me digging a deeper hole for myself, because how the F do you explain away what you "meant" when what came out of your mouth was something from *Return of the Super Bitch*?

She handled both my comment and my groveling with a very admirable amount of grace, laughing it off and assuring me her feelings weren't hurt. I didn't believe her for a second, but it was nice of her to say.

After several more extremely heartfelt (but what probably sounded like pathetically desperate) apologies, I bought the dress even though it cost way more than I wanted to spend. She made a hefty commission off of it, which seemed like the least I could do.

Parting Thoughts

When I was thirteen, I was visiting extended family for the summer (sans my parents, who were back at home). One traumatizing Friday late in the summer, I got my first period. Convinced there was something gravely wrong and I was dying, I asked my grandmother for help. She got me all sorted out and then promptly and exuberantly called my mom and dad to tell them the news, at which point my dad said to me, "Congratulations, sweetie! You're a woman now!" It was a conversation of such epic embarrassment and awkwardness that to this day I cringe to replay it in my head.

Gramma and I were supposed to head to a lakeside party that night with several other family members and some of their friends. Despite my fervent pleas to bow out for the evening, we went. The evening quickly turned into an impromptu "Congratulations, you're a woman now!" party as the news of my womanhood spread among the enthusiastic guests. They all meant well, but as you accept congratulations (and "I remember the day I got my first period!" commiseration stories) from multiple family friends, cousins, and people you don't even know, you slowly realize that everyone there knows that you're now capable of reproduction. The level of teenage horror one feels in this situation is unmatched.

There was even a cake. I'll let you guess what color it was.

Looking back, yeah, it's a funny story—but then? Words cannot describe.

Since then, I've been in many, many (many) more awkward and embarrassing situations—mostly of my own making—and would like to think that I'm getting better at handling them when they come up. But as my life continues, I regularly encounter situations that reset the bar for awkward—which is something I've realized I savor.

As awkward and embarrassing as it might feel in the moment, I hope these situations never stop: What fun is life if you have everything figured out? And besides that, part of what makes life great is suffering through these less-than-ideal moments so we can better appreciate the good moments when they pop up.

So, when life hurls a watermelon-sized lemon at your face, hopefully the glorious tome you hold in your hands has not only taught you to make a damn good lemon-drop martini, but to serve it with the grace, confidence, charm, and inherent know-how of a savvy White House-party crasher.

(Or at least I hope it has. ☺)

Yours in slapping awkward down,
S

Acknowledgments

Thank you, thank you, THANK YOU to the entire team at The Experiment: To Matthew Lore and Karen Giangreco for your ideas, enthusiasm, and superior editing skills. To Polly Watson for your copyediting savvy and Kathryn Williams for proofreading—I know I made you earn your keep. To Alison Forner for designing the cover, and to Pauline Neuwirth for setting my words in a way cool design. To Eliot Lucas for making my stories come alive in some truly awesome cartoons. And to Rose Carrano for your PR know-how and to Maribeth Casey for spreading *Awkward* around the world.

A HUGE thank-you to my fans and friends for your unending support, and especially to these people for letting me steal your quotes and stories, for the belly-laughs, and for tirelessly re-positioning my book to the best-seller table: Brad Bulkley, Whitman Dewey-Smith, Jennifer Fitzpatrick, Raymond Flotat, Brian Fulkerson, Jane Gooding, Ben Hirashima, David Hobbet, Kimberly Irion, Lindsay Johnson, Pamela, Lowell and Josiah Jones, Jun Kamata, Kevin Kirn, Kris Lande, the Lawson/Weil family, Ryan Lewis, Jeremy Malasky, Courtney McAra, the S.O. Book Club, Jennifer McMahon, Kirk Moore, Yvonne Nguyen, L. David Peters, Micah Rowland, the Seattle 20s and 30s Women Fiction Writers, Bekkah Schear, Rebecca Schenker, Georgina Seabrook, Mona Seymour, Kimberly Shin, Erin Snow, Courtney Stovall, Sarah Tharp, Leslie Thornton, Dan Vandervelde, Lindsay Wood, and my entire eternally optimistic and supportive family—most notably Mary Lynn Rutledge, Pamela Scholfield, James Scholfield, Megs Booker, Niall Booker, Jack and Lucille Scholfield, and KT, Brandon, and Eric Repp.

To the Gooding & Company family (including the seriously corrupted circus geek, TJ Simons—I told you I'd put it in!)—my life is forever changed for the better for knowing all of you, and our collective debauchery holds a very special place in my heart. Thank you for your support, the awkwardness, the impropriety, the ill-advised late nights and tequila shots, and the memories. You guys are amazing.

A very special thanks to Emily Benowitz, Tegan Kaske, Eagle Jones, and Lindsay Wood for their phenomenal feedback and suggestions. Without you, this book would suck a lot more. (P.S. I will forever treasure the "haha" comments in the margins, as well as this note: "Seriously, Sam, there must be something wrong with you. This shit doesn't happen to people unless they're in sitcoms.")

And most especially to Eagle—the most amazing boyfriend ever—thank you for listening to my endless ramble of ideas, helping me brainstorm, editing (and re-editing and re-re-editing) with a very skilled red pen, calling me out on my crazy, making me laugh, and supporting me in too many ways to list. You're absolutely amazing, and I love you.

To the many, many people—both those I've known and those I haven't—in coffee shops, on the street, in bars, at parties, on airplanes, in restaurants, in cars, and pretty much everywhere else who I've eavesdropped on, observed, and interacted with—you've given me some wildly delicious material to work with. From the bottom of my heart: Thank you.

And if you read this book? Thank you! You're obviously extremely intelligent, breathtakingly attractive, and have excellent taste. You're also awesome. I hope you enjoyed it.

259

About the Author

Samantha Scholfield is a frequent contributor to Yahoo.com and has offered her expertise through *Seventeen, Cosmopolitan,* and *The Huffington Post.* She has degrees from UCLA in English Literature and Bio-Geography (useful only at trivia nights and for blurting random facts at cocktail parties), dabbles in thinking about maybe training for triathlons, and has recently discovered the stress-relieving joys of zombie video games. She lives in San Francisco with her boyfriend and a houseplant named Bob. This is her second book.

www.awkwardsurvivalguide.com
www.samanthascholfield.com

About the Illustrator

Eliot Lucas has been drawing for as long as he can remember. He holds a BA in graphic design from Northern State University and has worked as a graphic designer since 2007, focusing on print and interactive media and continuing to explore painting and the fine arts. He is the creator of the online comic Whatever (www.whatevercomic.com), which he began in 2001. In his free time, Eliot enjoys acting and has appeared in independent films as well as stage productions. He lives with his cat Phoebe in Aberdeen, South Dakota.